Decorative
DOUGH *for*
CELEBRATIONS

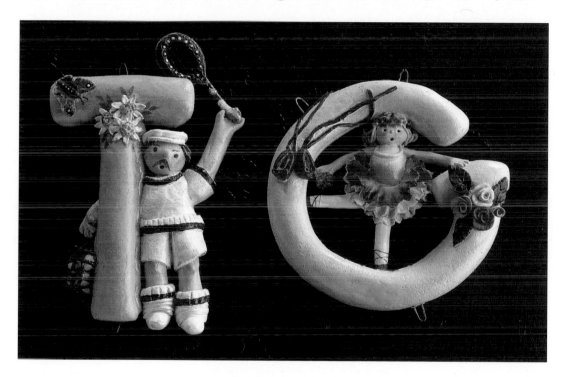

JOANNA JONES

MEREHURST

To those two great scholars — my sister,
Sally Wathen, and the Governor — with love.

ACKNOWLEDGEMENT
My thanks to Maisie Blackburn and her staff, Blackburns,
Cake Decorations and Craft Equipment, 108, Alexandra
Drive, Surbiton, Surrey, KT5 9AG, who are extremely
helpful and will usually send equipment to any destination.

Published in 1995 by
Merehurst Limited, Ferry House, 51–57 Lacy Road,
Putney, London SW15 1PR

A catalogue record of this book is available from the
British Library.

Edited by Bridget Jones
Designed by Maggie Aldred
Photography by James Duncan

Typeset by J&L Composition Ltd, Filey, North Yorkshire
Colour separation and Printing by
Toppan, Singapore

CONTENTS

~

INTRODUCTION

I only ever had one lesson on dough modelling and that was an impromptu affair, delivered by a wheelchair-bound American lady in the middle of Harrods' book department. The information was, of necessity, brief and strictly verbal, but I managed to scribble a few notes down on the back of an envelope before her irascible husband wheeled her away in mid-flow. Nevertheless, she did manage to fish a tube of hand cream from her handbag as she sped along and she threw this to me before eventually being engulfed in a lift. She was still saying *something* to me when the closing doors finally hid her from view, but it was several years before I could guess what she was saying, or before I learnt the significance of the hand cream. It did not matter, though, because at last I had the precious salt dough recipe for which I had been, quite literally, searching for years.

This may seem hard to believe now, when almost every week magazines print dough projects and there are several books available on the subject, but not very long ago there was absolutely no information to be had anywhere. So you can imagine the excitement with which I carried the scribbled notes home and the fervour with which I threw myself into my new craft.

The only piece of dough modelling I had ever seen, and the piece that had inspired me in the first place, was a rather sturdy, rustic figure. So to begin with I gave my dough dollies the same generous proportions. Even when I started to swap their smocks and aprons for delicately patterned dresses and petticoats, they still retained their ample hips and tree-trunk legs and looked like peasants dressed in their Sunday best. At the time, I thought they were absolutely stunning and confidently took them to shops and craft fairs where they sold surprisingly well. It must have been their rarity value that sold them though, because, quite frankly, the one or two that have survived from that period are huge and absolutely horrible.

It was not until I began to make very small figures to fit onto initials that I realized how grotesque the original forms were and I began to look for ways to slim them down. The main problem seemed to be that I had been trying to be too literal and cram too much clothing on the characters. Whereas originally I fitted them out with the complete, tailor-made works, adding similar lines and may be used for a variety of different effects. To make hair, fit one of the sieve-like discs into the end of the gun and load the tube with slightly dampened dough.

Pull the trigger to push strands of dough out onto a lightly floured board. Then use floured plastic tweezers to pick up little clumps of hair and transfer these to the dampened head.

Clay-gun hair is usually much finer than garlic-press hair and with care it can be extruded in waves, straight onto the head. It can also be coaxed into curls after it has been arranged on the head by using a cocktail stick (toothpick) or modelling tool.

Fine sieve I use this method of making hair for short, male styles, for little dolls and for a permed effect.

Soften the dough slightly with a little water and, using the back of a wooden

Pushing dough through a fine sieve to make hair.

spoon, push it through the sieve. The longer you work away with the spoon, the longer the hair on the other side of the sieve will grow, but as this method gives a very compact effect it is best to reserve it for short styles.

Remove the hair from the back of the sieve with a sharp knife and transfer it directly to the head.

Curls For creatures such as cherubs, who simply must have big fat curls, the only solution is to roll them by hand.

Make several very small tapering ropes about 12mm ($\frac{1}{2}$in) in length and, starting at one end, roll each rope into a coil. Dot these all over the head at different angles; I usually reserve one, which is coming slightly uncurled, for the forehead.

MODELLING ARMS AND HANDS
Lay two suitable ropes of dough side by side on a floured board. Flatten the ends closest to you with a finger, then use a sharp knife to cut a small triangle of dough from the inside edge of each of the flattened pieces to represent the space between the thumb and the first finger.

Make three small cuts along the bottom edge of each piece to represent the fingers and trim these to the appropriate lengths. Using the sharp knife or a damp paint brush, carefully round the ends of the fingers and thumbs.

While the arms are still laying side by side, trim the tops of them diagonally so that the two diagonals form a 'V'; these slanting ends will eventually fit on either side of the body.

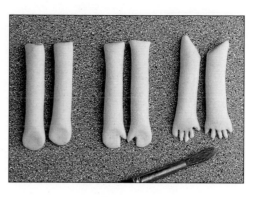

Modelling hands.

MAKING LEGS AND FEET
To make legs and feet that are wearing boots or shoes, lay two suitable ropes of dough together on a floured board. Leave the bottom ends of these ropes untrimmed so that they retain their rounded appearance.

Lay a finger across one of the ropes, about 12mm ($\frac{1}{2}$in) from the rounded end, and roll the rope very gently to make a slight indentation. Dab a spot of water on the indentation and then bend the rounded end up at right angles to form a foot. Make the other foot in the same way.

If you wish to give the appearance of boots, fix a very thin rope of dough around each leg, just above the ankle or halfway up the calf.

To make legs with bare feet, lay the ropes side by side as before, but trim both bottom ends diagonally so that together they form a 'V'. Make four small cuts along the diagonal edges to represent toes and round each toe off, either with a sharp knife or a damp brush. As bare feet are generally used on flying angels or cherubs I do not usually bend them at the ankle, but if you want that effect treat them as above.

While the legs are still together, trim the top ends diagonally so that together they form a 'V'; these diagonals fit on either side of the body.

MAKING A BOW

Cut two long, narrow strips of dough. Cut a quarter of the length from one and cut the other in half diagonally. Take the diagonally cut pieces and notch both the straight ends before fixing the diagonal ends together on the model.

Loop both ends of the longest remaining piece towards the middle and fix together in the centre. Wrap the last

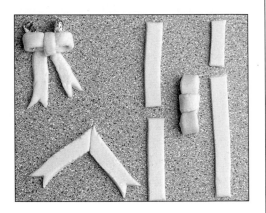

Making a bow.

short piece around the middle to represent the knot and fix together at the back. Arrange the bow in the middle of the ribbon tails. Fill the loops with some crushed silver foil, if necessary, to support their shape during baking.

Note You may like to use a plastic strip cutter instead of a knife to get all the strips looking exactly the same. These are available in sugarcraft shops.

MAKING A FRILL

Use a fluted round cutter of a suitable size to cut out a circle of thinly rolled dough. Use a smaller round cutter to remove the centre of the fluted circle.

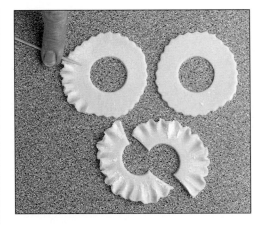

Making a frill.

Using a cocktail stick (toothpick) like a very small rolling pin, roll out each of the flutes around the circle, with a gentle rocking motion. Flour the cocktail stick repeatedly while you work. When you have frilled the complete ring, cut it into the required lengths.

MAKING A SITTING CAT

Make two slim ropes of dough for the front legs and lay them side by side on a floured board. Make three small cuts along the front edge of both to represent the toes. Round each of these individually with a damp paint brush. Trim the other end of each leg diagonally and fix together with a little water.

Place a small pear-shaped piece of dough on top of the legs, tapered end to the front, so that about half the legs

are still protruding. Make a small ball of dough for the head and add a very small triangular wedge of dough for the nose.

Add two very small flattened balls of dough close to the nose, to represent whisker pads. Fix the head in place. Make two pointed ears by cutting a small circle with a small round cutter and quartering it. Flatten two of these quarters a little and fit them to the top of the cat's head. Fix a thin tapering rope of dough on the rear of the cat and then curl it around the body

Note If you want to attach the cat's head at a particularly awkard angle, water alone might not be enough. Take a short length of wire and push half into the head and half into the body to reinforce the join.

MAKING A BUTTERFLY

Using the butterfly cutter, stamp the shape out of thinly rolled dough and lay it on a lightly floured board. Use a cocktail stick (toothpick) to flute the outside edges of the wings, as when making a frill, then fix the butterfly on the project with a little water. Roll a very small cigar-shaped body and fix this between the two wings.

Wet the sides of the body a little and push the wings up so that they adhere to it. If the wings droop, then support them in an upright position by tucking two small rolls of foil underneath them during baking. Trim two black stamens to the right length and push these into the front of the body to represent antennae.

To make a very small butterfly, cut out two heart shapes and trim off the pointed ends. Stick these wings on either side of a small cigar-shaped body and support them with foil if necessary. Small butterflies look better if you paint their antennae in front of their heads on the main dough model after it is baked.

MODELLING BIRDS

Doves Take a small ball of well-kneaded dough and pull out one side slightly. Model this into a rounded head with a pinched-in neck and a small beak.

Flatten the other end of the dough into a fan-shaped tail, pinching it in at the base. Tip the tail up slightly and make three or four small cuts along the edge to represent tail feathers.

Use a small leaf cutter to make two wings and feather these with the back of a knife. Finish using a cocktail stick (toothpick) to indent two eyes in the dough.

Robin Make the head, wings and beak as for the dove, but instead of making a fan-shaped tail, pull the dough out to a point to suggest long tail feathers.

Pigeon Start the pigeon in a similar way to the dove, but make the head smaller and the body streamlined, ending in a tail like the one on the robin.

If the pigeon is very big, make thin wings with a leaf cutter, but if it is quite small it will look better with painted wings, added after baking.

MAKING ROSES AND ROSEBUDS

I generally use the two smallest cutters in a small set of round cutters; the set is sometimes sold as a 'Briar Rose' set.

Cut out two small circles and two larger ones from thinly rolled dough. Cut all the circles in half and flatten them slightly to make the edges as thin as possible.

Take one of the smaller semi-circles and, starting at one corner, roll the dough into a coil to resemble the centre of a rose. Fix the end with a little water. You may leave some pieces at this stage to represent rosebuds.

Dampen the longest edges of the three small semi-circles before wrapping them evenly around the bud, overlapping them to make them fit. At this stage the roses may be used as small flowers. Add the final four large semi-circles in the same way to make full-blown roses.

VEINING LEAVES

There are cutters available for making a wide variety of leaves, but the most useful is the rose leaf which can usually double up for other types.

To vein the rose leaf, use the back of a knife to mark a central vein and then add four or five pairs of smaller veins coming from it.

Leaves like ivy and holly have such distinctive shapes that you really have to buy the proper cutter. Use the back of a knife to give both of them a central vein only. The ivy cutter will also double for a grape vine leaf.

MAKING FLOWERS WITH A PRIMROSE CUTTER

The primrose cutter is another very versatile piece of equipment which can be used to make a variety of other flowers.

Primrose or Primula Cut the shape out of thinly rolled dough and fix the flower in position, then make a hole in the middle with the pointed end of a modelling tool. This will give a deep, wide hole which will look quite realistic when painted.

Christmas Rose Cut out a flower and lay it in the palm of your hand, then gently press each petal with the rounded end of a modelling tool to thin and slightly cup the petals. Fix the flower in position and fill the centres with five shortened stamens.

Dog Rose Make the flowers as for Christmas rose, but use slightly longer stamens. The main difference is in the painting.

DAISIES

Daisy cutters usually come in sets of three, so you can make anything from a small daisy to a large Marguerite.

Lay the cut-out flower on a thin piece of foam rubber and press each petal with the small leaf-shaped end of a modelling tool. Pull the tool back slightly as you do this and it will have the effect of curving the edges of each petal towards each other. Place a small flattened ball of dough in the centre of the daisy and prick this all over with a cocktail stick.

MAKING HANGING HOOKS

The most successful hanging hooks are made from traditional hairpins. Trim them to length, as necessary for your project, using wire cutters. The trimmings from the straight-sided pins may be bent into hooks as well.

Painting and Varnishing

Painting brings dough models to life and makes them look interesting. Unfortunately, most of the models you see for sale have been painted with unsuitable paints and the results are crude. Treat yourself to professional paints and brushes and give up any ideas of a trial run with the children's paint box and a cosmetic brush!

You could use two or three old saucers instead of a palette, but a 'Chrysanthemum' palette is the most useful and china will not stain in the same way as plastic. Paints, brushes, palettes and spirit-based acrylic varnish are all available in the art shop, but go to a do-it-yourself store to purchase oil-based polyurethane varnish.

Absorbent paper is handy for wiping brushes and to lay your model on while you are painting. I also have a sharp craft knife and some cotton buds so that I can erase the inevitable mistake, wiping it off with the bud or scraping it off with the knife.

For bread dough you will also need a chunk of polystyrene (styrofoam) of the kind used for packaging or flower arranging and hand cream which should be as non sticky as possible.

PAINTS

Water Colours These come in small cakes or tubes and they give a transparent finish. They are perfectly alright for dough modelling; however, and I use them if I want to preserve the look of natural salt dough with just a gentle wash of colour. I use water colours mostly on bread dough where it can be blended to get the most delicate and realistic effects, especially on flowers.

Acrylic paints In my opinion, acrylic paints are not suitable for dough modelling. Their natural tendency to dry quickly is accentuated by the porous quality of both salt dough and bread dough. This gives rise to patchiness and makes blending impossible.

Craft paints These are the little pots of ready-mixed paints for craft workers. Provided that they are water based and non-acrylic, these are fine for dough and are especially good if you do not have the confidence to mix colours.

Poster paints It is possible to use these on dough, but the results tend to be rather garish and powdery.

Gouache Paints or Designer Colours These are the paints that I use most; so, of course, you would not expect me to say anything but good about them. They come in a range of traditional colours and are perfect for dough modellers. They can be used in an opaque way or watered down and they allow plenty of time for blending.

Brushes The rough surface of salt dough is very hard on brushes, therefore I would advise you mainly to use artists' synthetic brushes material. These lose their points very quickly though, so it is useful to buy one or two of the more expensive sable brushes for occasions when a fine point is essential. Sables are also the best brushes to use on bread dough which does not wear them out as quickly as salt dough.

VARNISHES

Salt dough is extremely susceptible to damp and has to be varnished with quite strong varnish to seal it. A good-quality clear, gloss, oil-based polyurethane varnish is best. The sparkle varnishing gives to your work more than compensates for the slight yellowing it may cause.

Do not use a water-based acrylic varnish, even if it does say 'polyurethane' on the tin. Although this does not cause yellowing, being water based it will smudge your painting and ruin it. It is often advisable to use a stronger sealant, such as yacht varnish, on bowls or other pieces that are going to be used and handled a lot. Since this varnish gives an even more yellow finish, use darker colours when painting.

Keep a small soft brush solely for applying varnish and clean it in turpentine or white spirits (mineral spirits), before rinsing it in warm, soapy water.

Bread dough may be varnished with artists' quality, *spirit-based*, acrylic varnish which is clear and quick drying. This varnish is not as strong as polyurethane, but it has the advantage of not yellowing.

Paint Terms and Techniques

Pure This means the colour as it comes from the tube with *just* enough water added to make it flow.

Watery or thin Mix the paint with more water than usual, but stop short of making it transparent.

Transparent Mix the paint with so much water that you are adding just a suggestion of colour to the dough.

Wash A wash is a transparent layer of paint. This sometimes refers to a thin application of paint over a thicker one.

PAINTING FACES
Start the doll's face by painting on some flesh colour and then, while this is still damp, mix a little more Cadmium Red into part of the mixture to get a pink. Work this into the doll's cheeks so that it blends gently into the background colour. If you find this difficult, take a clean damp brush and blend with that. Reserve some of the mixture when you are making the pink, in case you need to return to it for making corrections.

For a standard dough dolly, whose eyes and mouth have been made with a cocktail stick, run a little pale blue around the inside of the eye holes and some mid-pink around the inside of the mouth to complete the face. Sometimes it also looks good to blend a touch of pink onto the fingertips and toes, especially with angels, children and cherubs.

In cases where you have only modelled the nose and have left the eyes and mouth blank, start off in the same way by painting the flesh colour and blending the cheeks, and then continue by painting two very pale blue almonds for the

eyes. When dry, encircle the almond shapes with thin black lines and paint in any eyelashes and eyebrows.

Paint a coloured iris in each eye and choose the position and size of them to give expression. Small irises surrounded by white look amazed, whereas large ones painted towards the corners can look quite sultry. When the irises are dry, surround them with a thin black line and paint a small black dot in the middle.

Use a medium pink for the mouth, making it a little browner if your subject is a man and a bright lipstick colour if you are painting that sort of girl. Mouths can add volumes to the personality of the face, but paint the central line between lips with the most care as you can make someone look very jolly or utterly miserable, depending on whether the corners turn up or down. Finally, add moustaches, beauty spots or eye shadow.

PAINTING PATTERNS
Paint the base colour and allow to dry.

Spots and dots Use the tip of your brush to paint evenly spaced dots of a similar size all over the base colour. If you are feeling more adventurous, you might like to consider larger spots with golden circles painted around them. These look particularly good on a clown's outfit or a ballet dancer's skirt.

Tartans Use your rigger brush and the main colour to use as a background. When dry, paint some horizontal lines in broad strokes, leaving enough room

Using a rigger brush to paint stripes.

between the strokes to paint in another line later. Paint similar vertical lines in the same colour.

Then, holding your rigger up on end to produce a thinner stroke, paint a different colour between all the previous lines; horizontally and vertically.

For a more complicated tartan effect, you may also paint a very thin line down the middle of all the broad lines: this works particularly well in black.

FLOWERED PATTERNS
To produce a very simple daisy petal, hold an artists' brush on its point and move it back slowly while allowng more and more of the brush to touch the surface. Complete the stroke by lifting the brush back onto its point and away from the work. Practise this stroke on paper first and then, when you have perfected it, make several widely spaced dots over the area that you want to cover and encircle each with a ring of daisy petals. For a variation, put single polka dots among the flowers.

13

PAINTS USED FOR PROJECTS

	Mother Hen	Thanksgiving Sheaf	Thanksgiving Wreath	Thanksgiving Place Names	Candelabra	Christmas Wreath	Nativity Scene	Carol Singers	Festive Table Centrepiece	Christmas Place Names	Christmas Napkin Rings	Bread Dough Napkin Rings	Rocking Horse	Christmas Stockings	Father Christmas	Christmas Tree Angel	Christmas Labels	Cherubs and Hearts	Valentine's Day Mirror	Mother's Day Flowers	Halloween Witch
Lemon Yellow	●			●		●			●								●	●	●	●	
Cadmium Yellow			●	●		●	●	●						●	●	●				●	●
Yellow Ochre							●	●						●							
Ultramarine	●			●		●	●	●						●		●		●	●	●	
Olive Green				●				●	●	●	●	●			●		●	●	●	●	
Fir Green						●		●					●	●							
Viridian					●																●
Saffron Green														●							
Linden Green				●					●			●									
Rose Madder																			●		
Cadmium Red	●		●	●		●	●	●	●			●		●	●	●				●	●
Rose Pink														●	●			●			
Alizarin Crimson		●														●					
Red Ochre							●														
Spectrum Red						●					●	●					●				
Flame Red													●	●	●						
Magenta								●													●
Spectrum Violet				●				●												●	
Burnt Sienna	●						●	●													
Raw Umber						●											●				●
Jet Black	●	●	●	●			●	●	●					●	●	●	●				●
Permanent White	●				●	●	●	●						●	●	●	●	●	●	●	●
Silver																					
Gold				●		●	●	●						●	●	●	●	●	●		●

14

THE CRACKING PROBLEM

● Cracking is the bane of a dough modeller's life and even though there does not seem to be a clear-cut solution, there are some tips which might help. Do not model with dough that is too soft, because it has a tendency to dent and cracks form along the dents as it dries. Soft dough can be caused by too much water or by too little salt.

● Make sure that you knead your dough thoroughly so that no air remains; trapped air expands in the oven and it then cracks the dough.

● If the dough is too dry, it will actually be covered in minute cracks before baking, and these will inevitably expand in the heat.

● I have added *a little* oil to the basic dough mixture to help alleviate the problem of cracking, but do not be tempted to add more oil as the dough will then take hours longer to bake and end up stuck to the baking tray. You will then probably still crack it, trying to prise it off!

● Cook dough at as low a temperature, and for as long as, possible; in fact, you should think of the process as 'drying' rather than 'cooking'. I have given good average times and settings for drying the dough, but if you are willing to experiment with your oven, you may find that leaving the dough in for a much longer time at a lower setting will avoid the problem of cracking.

● Leave the dough in the oven to cool down slowly after it has cooked and you have turned off the heat.

● To repair a crack quickly, fill it with a hard-drying glue and use reasonably thick paint to cover the glue. Alternatively, fill it with soft dough, then smooth it over and bake it again. Rub it down with fine sandpaper before painting. You may also use fine surface filler and follow the instructions on the packet.

Ballet Dancer Initial	Tennis Player Initial	Gingerbread Men and Women	Birthday Labels	Engagement Bowl	Bridal Couple	Mother and Baby with Pram	Nanny and Baby Rabbit	House with Georgian Door	Town House	Tree Decorations and Tags:	Walking Sticks, page 40	Christmas Tree, page 42	Christmas Puddings, page 45	Gift Tags, page 56
•	•				•	•								
•	•		•		•	•		•	•					•
•	•	•	•	•		•	•	•	•			•	•	•
•	•		•	•		•		•	•		•	•		•
														•
		•							•					
												•		
				•	•									•
•	•	•	•		•	•		•	•					•
												•		
					•		•		•					
		•				•		•						
											•			
								•					•	
								•						
	•								•			•		
	•							•	•				•	
	•		•			•	•	•				•		•
	•	•	•		•	•	•	•	•				•	•
•	•	•	•	•	•	•	•	•	•			•	•	•
	•				•									
			•		•				•			•	•	•

FESTIVE OCCASIONS

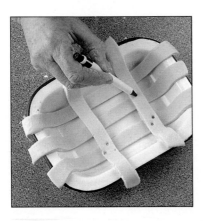

Making dots to represent nails on the strips of dough.

It somehow seems fitting that we should make gifts and decorations for ancient festivals with a material as old and as basic as dough. In fact, some things, such as the wheat sheaf and the nativity scene, have been traditionally made in dough of one kind or another for centuries. It is also good to include a few ideas from this era and you might consider making a dough table centre and matching napkin rings for Christmas or Thanksgiving. Those with a sense of humour may like to make wicked dough portraits of guests with gingerbread cutters. If you use these instead of place names it should break the ice quicker than any brandy punch!

· MOTHER HEN ·

20 × 15cm (8 × 6in) pie dish
vegetable oil
¾ quantity Basic Dough, see page 6
plastic ruler
retracted ballpoint pen
garlic press or clay gun
rose petal cutter
modelling tool
small bird cutter
cocktail stick (toothpick)
Egg Glaze, see page 7
poppy seeds
50cm (20in) yellow ribbon

1 Thoroughly coat the inside and the lip of the pie dish with oil and put it to one side. Roll out about a third of the dough to 6mm (¼in

thick. Then use a well-floured plastic ruler and a sharp knife to cut three strips measuring about 22.5 × 2cm (9 × ¾in). Lay these lengthways, evenly spaced, along the bottom of the dish so that they reach up the sides with their ends resting on the lip.

2 Cut two 17.5 × 2cm (7 × ¾in) strips and lay them at right angles over the first strips. Dab a little water where the two sets of strips cross and then mark a couple of dots on the junctions to represent nails.

3 Take a good handful of dough and roll a finger-thick 70cm (28in) long rope. Dampen the ends of all the strips and then, starting at one corner, fit the roll around the top of the pie dish. Flatten the roll slightly with your fingers and make 'nail' marks with the ballpoint pen wherever it crosses the end of a strip.

4 From now on, as you work, prop up the pie dish slightly on one long side, so that you can get a better idea of what the design will look like when it is finished and hanging on the wall. Use the clay gun or garlic press to build up a good nest of 'straw' in the bottom half of the dish. The straw should stretch from side to side and reach up about as far as the middle strip.

5 Model a small handful of dough into a tear-drop shape for the hen's body. Make a few feather-like shapes on the chest and back of the body by using a small metal tube, like the cap of an eyebrow pencil or something similar, to indent the dough at an angle while lifting it slightly. This will create small flaps of dough that resemble feathers.

Mother Hen

Using a small metal tube to mark feather-like shapes on the bird's chest.

6 To make the wings, roll out a small amount of dough thinly and cut out two leaves with the rose leaf cutter. Starting close to the pointed ends, cut two notches along one side of each leaf. Fix these on the hen's body, rounded ends to the front and the notched sides uppermost.

7 Sit the hen in the straw, then model an oval shape for the head. Pull a small, pointed piece of dough out at one end of the oval to represent a beak and then fix the head onto the body, so that she appears to be looking back over her shoulder.

8 Flatten four small balls of dough and arrange these in a line along the top of the hen's head to represent her comb. Flatten another ball of dough, cut it in half and fix it under her chin.

9 Mould three small pear-shaped pieces of dough for the chicks and pinch the narrow ends into little tails. Make three small balls for heads and pull a small pointed piece of dough out on one side of each for a beak.

10 Fix the heads onto the bodies and place two chicks in the straw behind the mother hen, and one in front of her. Use a cocktail stick (toothpick) to mark eyes on the hen and her chicks.

11 Roll a fairly small ball of dough and hollow out the middle with the rounded end of a modelling tool to make a small bowl shape. Place this in the straw towards the back of the dish.

12 Use the small bird cutter to indent a design on the long sides of the rim, marking a bird between each set of nails.

13 Model 24 small eggs and place two of these just under the hen. Arrange the rest in pairs to complete the decoration on the rim.

14 Paint the dish with the egg glaze, but do not paint the hen, chicks and bowl. Drip a little glaze into the bottom of the bowl and sprinkle some poppy seeds onto it. Bake at 145°C (290°F/Gas 1½) for about 2 hours.

Painting and Finishing

● Mix a little white into some Burnt Sienna to make a warm light brown. Paint the hen with this and before it has a chance to dry, add a little more white to the mixture and paint little arcs of colour onto her chest feathers.

Use the same colour to suggest a double line of feathers on either side of her face and to draw a couple of curving lines under her eyes. Use Jet Black to accentuate her eyes and to paint some feathery shapes on the top half of her back and the rounded end of her wings. Add a line of Cadmium Red dots to the feather patterns on her back and wing, and use the same colour to paint the comb and chin piece.

Use some pure Lemon Yellow to paint the beak and add a little white to this to get the colour for the chicks. While the pale yellow is still damp on the chicks, add a little watery Cadmium Red to their cheeks. Add a tiny speck of red to the pale yellow to get a pale orange for their little beaks. Dot their eyes with Jet Black and draw two curved lines in pale brown on their sides to suggest wings. Paint the decorative birds on the rim of the dish in the same way.

Mix some Ultramarine and white together to make the pale blue for the bowl and paint this carefully so as not to get paint on the poppy seeds. When the bowl is quite dry, decorate the rim and sides with two slightly darker blue lines. Finally, paint all the eggs white.

Varnish in the usual way and allow to dry. Loop a piece of yellow ribbon loosely around the two strips at the rear of the hen house. Tie the ends in a firm bow at the front and hang the house by the slack ribbon at the back.

·THANKSGIVING SHEAF·

The Thanksgiving sheaf is made to a traditional design with origins in the mists of time, probably as far back as pagan times, when bread was often baked in ritual shapes and offered to the gods in the hope of a good harvest. Little is known about the early artistic history of bread and we are not sure when a more durable, but inedible, recipe for dough was made, so that the bakers' efforts would survive to become cherished ornaments.

1½ quantities Basic Dough, see page 6
Egg Glaze, see page 7
15cm (6in) saucer
nail scissors • modelling tool
very fine floristry wire
cocktail stick (toothpick)
1 hairpin
1m (40in) orange ribbon

1   Roll out about a quarter of the dough to 6mm (¼in) thick. Using the saucer as a template, cut out a circle of dough and place it at one end of a baking tray. Cut a 12.5 × 7.5cm (5 × 3in) rectangle of dough and fix this on the circle so that it overlaps by about 12mm (½in) to resemble a lollipop with a fat stick.

2   Take a handful of dough and roll out a 30cm (12in) long pencil-thin rope, leaving 5cm (2in) at one end about twice as thick. Lay this down the middle of the lollipop shape so that it overhangs by about 2.5cm (1in) at the fat end and 6mm (¼in) at the thin end.

3   Use scissors to make a row of nicks around the base of the fat end to represent an ear of corn. Snip a second row behind the first and continue until the whole ear of corn is complete. Make fourteen more ears of corn and arrange them symmetrically on either side of

the first one to completely cover the base. Some of the circle will still be showing, but this will be covered by the next layer of corn.

4   Make fifteen more ears of corn, this time making them 22.5cm (9in) long. Pile these on top of the first layer so that their tops are about 4cm (1½in) lower and with some of their heads drooping down to cover the rest of the circle. When all the stalks are in place and all the heads are nicked, pinch the dough in as though the corn is bound in a sheaf.

5   To make the body of the mouse, mould a

Thanksgiving Sheaf

Making ears of corn

19

Laying the ears of corn on the wreath.

Putting on the second set of ropes.

CRAFT TIP

You may secure the decorations if you wish but you will notice that I have fixed both the ribbon and the flowers with Blu-Tack, so that they can be removed easily when they get dusty or when you simply wish to ring the changes.

small handful of dough into a pear shape. Fix this on the ears of corn with a little water. Make two ears by indenting two small balls of dough with the round end of a modelling tool. Arrange these on top of the mouse's head and mark the eyes with a cocktail stick (toothpick). Cut the floristry wire into six short lengths and stick three of them into the dough on either side of his nose. Finally, roll a thin tapering tail of dough and arrange it so that it curls out across the dough behind the mouse.

6 Fix the hairpin firmly in the top so that most of it is embedded in the dough. Paint the sheaf all over with egg glaze. Bake at 145°C (290°F/Gas $1\frac{1}{2}$) for 3 to 4 hours, brushing with more glaze once or twice for a rich colour.

Painting and Finishing

● Make up some watery Alizarin and wash it onto the mouse's tail, ears and nose. Then use Jet Black to mark his eyes and whiskers. Varnish and decorate with a ribbon when dry.

THANKSGIVING · WREATH ·

$1\frac{1}{2}$ quantities Basic Dough, see page 6
25cm (10in) plate
15cm (6in) saucer · nail scissors
fine floristry wire
cocktail stick (toothpick)
large plastic drinking straw
wide strip cutter
Egg Glaze, see page 7
Hanging Hook, see page 11
2m ($2\frac{1}{4}$yd) ribbon · Blu-Tack
small bunch of dried flowers (optional)

1 Roll out a third of the dough to 6mm ($\frac{1}{4}$in) thick. Using the larger plate as a template, cut out a circle of dough and place it on a baking tray. Position the saucer in the middle of the circle and use that as a template to cut out the centre.

2 Gather up any scraps of dough and knead them back into the main ball of dough. Roll eight thin 10cm (4in) long ropes of dough and lay them side by side and diagonally over the bottom of the dough ring. Tuck the ends under the ring and secure them in place with a little water.

3 Make seven similar ropes and model ears of corn, see page 19. Trim two to 17.5cm (7in) and 15cm (6in), and five to 12.5cm (5in). Take the longest one first and arrange it at a slant, so that the stalk lays over the first group of ropes, slanting in the opposite direction and about one third of the way along from the inside edge. Tuck the stalk under the inside of the ring and allow the head to lay on the baking tray. Arrange the 15cm (6 in) stalk in a similar manner, laying it close to the first. Arrange two of the remaining stalks on either side and secure the last three on top, with two of them curving outwards. When you have finished this arrangement there should still be at least half of the first group of ropes showing.

4 Roll a second set of eight ropes and lay these in a similar way to the first set, working on the opposite slant and starting off by covering the exposed corner of the original ropes. Make a further set of ropes, this time making the eighth one complete with an ear of wheat. Lay these in place diagonally, in the opposite direction to the previous set and so that they cover the foremost corner of it.

5 Work your way around the ring adding ropes of dough in this manner, always changing direction with each set and always covering the corner of the previous set. Work a head of corn into the groups occasionally for a

Thanksgiving Wreath

random effect. When you have worked your way back to the original group of stalks, lift the nearest head and tuck the free ends of the last set of ropes underneath.

6 Make five more stalks with heads and arrange these so that their stalks lay over the first set, facing in the opposite direction. Trim some of these last stalks quite short so that one or two of the ears of wheat lay on top of the wreath. Use the plastic drinking straw to make two holes right through the dough on the opposite side of the wreath to the corn. Model a mouse similar to the one on Thanksgiving Sheaf, see Step 5 on pages 19 and 20. Position it on one side of the wreath.

7 Roll out the rest of the dough to 3mm ($\frac{1}{8}$in) thick and use the wide strip cutter to cut out two 10cm (4in) long strips. Wrap these around the bunches of wheat at the bottom of the wreath so that they go between the two groups and tuck them under the edges of the wreath. Cut two more 10cm (4in) strips of dough and make a bow with long streamers, see page 10. Secure this on one of the binding strips and arrange the streamers so that they lay naturally on top of the ears of corn.

8 Finally, push a large hanging hook into the top of the wreath. Paint the whole wreath with the egg glaze and bake at 145°C (290°F/ Gas 1$\frac{1}{2}$) for about 3 hours. If you want a richer colour, continue to paint on egg glaze at regular intervals during the baking.

Painting and Finishing

Mix equal amounts of Cadmium Red and Yellow to make a bright orange and paint the binding ribbon and bow on the wreath.

Make some very watery Cadmium Red and wash a little of this onto the mouse's nose, tail and ear linings. Mark his eyes and paint his whiskers with Jet Black.

Adding colour to the bread dough.

Varnish the wreath in the usual way and allow it to dry. Cut the ribbon in two and notch one end of each piece. Push the notched ends through the holes at the top of the wreath and tie a bow on the front. Take one of the ends hanging from the back of the wreath and wrap the ribbon around the wreath once or twice, making sure that you avoid any stray ears of wheat and the mouse. Fix the end of the ribbon onto the back of the wreath with a piece of Blu-Tack just above the bunches of wheat. Wind the other end of ribbon around the other side of the wreath in a similar manner.

To decorate the wreath with dried flowers, push a fairly large piece of Blu-Tack onto the painted bow and stick the stalks of the dried flowers into this. Cut the stalks fairly short so that the heads cover the Blu-Tack.

BREAD DOUGH *THANKSGIVING* · PLACE NAMES ·

The design on these holders can also be used instead of the holly and Christmas roses on the Bread Dough Napkin Rings, see page 36. Together, the two sets provide rich trimmings for a Thanksgiving table, especially when complemented by bowls of fresh fruit.

$\frac{1}{2}$ quantity Bread Dough, see page 6
Olive Green gouache or water colour paint
waxed paper • plastic strip cutter
large and medium rose leaf cutters
black stamens • P.V.A. glue

1 Colour half the dough with Olive Green paint, see page 7. Shape half this dough into a round and roll it out between two sheets of waxed paper to 4mm ($\frac{5}{16}$in) thick. Press a medium-gauge plastic strip cutter into the dough so that it lightly marks it, then use the lines as a guide to cut out four 4cm × 8mm ($1\frac{1}{2}$ × $\frac{5}{8}$in) strips. Lay these ridged side up on a piece of waxed paper.

2　Roll out the remaining green dough thinly between two further sheets of waxed paper. Cut out eight large and eight medium rose leaves from the rolled out dough. Glue two of the larger leaves to the middle of the back of one of the ridged bases so that they overlap. Glue two of the smaller leaves to either end of the front of the base, laying on their sides with their points facing outerwards.

Decorate the other three bases in a similar way and then put them to one side to dry.

4　Use the remains of the white dough to make four small balls for limes, four medium balls for apples and four larger balls for oranges. Decorate each of these with the head of a stamen.

5　Model four balls of dough into pear shapes and stick part of the stem of a stamen into the narrow end of each of them to represent a stalk. Make about eighty tiny balls of dough to represent grapes and then put all the fruit on a piece of waxed paper to dry.

6　When the bases and the fruit have all dried, glue a pear, an apple, a lime and an orange on the front of each base, arranging them in a group. Leave enough room for a bunch of grapes and position the fruit high enough to support the name card in place.

7　Build up a bunch of about twenty grapes in the space and stick part of the stem of a stamen into this to represent the stalk. Leave the card holders until the glue is quite dry.

Painting and Finishing

● Paint the leaves and bases with pure Olive Green and dry thoroughly. Paint veins on the leaves with diluted Linden Green.

Wash thin Cadmium Yellow over the pears and while this is still wet, blend Linden Green around the stalk and stamen ends. Still working quickly into the damp paint, run streaks of thin Cadmium Red down each pear and soften it slightly with a clean damp brush.

Paint the apples and limes with pure Linden Green; while the apples are still wet paint several thin lines of watery Cadmium Red in patches around them. Blend the red lightly with a clean damp brush.

Mix Lemon Yellow and Cadmium Red together and use to paint the oranges. Then add a little Ultramarine to Spectrum violet and paint the grapes. Finish the stalks on the grapes and pears with pure Jet Black, and dab a little on all the stamens. Trim the edges of all the leaves with gold.

· CHRISTMAS WREATH ·

$1\frac{1}{4}$ quantities Basic Dough, see page 6
25cm (10in) plate
large holly leaf cutter
primrose cutter • stamens
large and small leaf cutters
cocktail stick (toothpick)
large plastic drinking straw
Hanging Hook, see page 11
1m (40in) red ribbon

1　Lay the plate on a baking tray and draw around it with a pencil. If the tray is very dark you may need to use a coloured pencil. Make a thick rope from half the dough, long enough to encircle the plate — about 70cm (28in). Lay the rope on the mark and join the ends by trimming each at an opposite slant and fixing them with water. Press the ring flat with your fingers until it is about 4cm ($1\frac{1}{2}$in) wide.

CRAFT TIP

Traditionally, holly wreaths are meant to be hung on the front door as a sign of welcome but unless you live in particularly sunny climes I would hang this dough wreath inside the house or it is likely to soften.

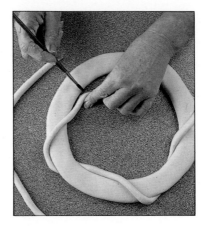

Draping a pencil-thin rope around the wreath.

FLESH COLOUR

To make flesh colour you need Permanent White, Cadmium Yellow and Cadmium Red. Take the white first and add a little water, then add a small amount of yellow and mix it in well. Follow this with a very small amount of the red and mix it in well. If the mixture looks too orange, add more white. The result should be a pale peach colour and definitely not pink or orange.

2 Make the arms and legs for the cherub, see page 11. Lay them at the top of the ring so that the finished cherub will cover the join, but do not secure the left hand. Model a generous pear shape for the body and lay this on the arms and legs. Separate the buttocks by making a line with the back of your knife.

3 Make a head with a smiling face, see page 49, and fix this facing forwards and resting on the left arm. Roll out some dough to 3mm ($\frac{1}{8}$in) thick and cut out two large leaves. Lay these together on the board and notch the outside edges of both to make a pair of wings. Fix the wings onto the cherub's back with the notched edge uppermost.

4 Make five pencil-thin ropes about 15cm (6in) long and drape these over and around the wreath so that they appear to be one continuous rope wound around it. Start the first one on the inside, just under the cherub's legs, and lay it diagonally across the wreath so that it finishes on the outside. Trim the ends of all the ropes at a slant so that they fit neatly against the sides of the wreath. Start the second rope on the inside and not quite opposite the first one and lay this across the wreath in the same way. Continue around the wreath in this fashion until the last rope ends close to the cherub's right hand.

5 Cut out 30 to 35 holly leaves and arrange these in groups of four or five on each of the ropes. Arrange similar groups between these, directly on the wreath, leaving a space of about 7.5cm (3in) at the bottom of the wreath. Make several holly berries from balls of dough and put three or four in the centre of each group of leaves. Place one berry in the left hand of the cherub, as if he is picking them.

6 Make a robin, see page 11, and sit him on the wreath close to, and facing, the cherub. Cut out about ten primroses and flatten their petals slightly, see page 11. Keeping the space at the bottom, place flowers symmetrically around the wreath. Push three shortened stamens into the centre of each.

7 Finally, use the drinking sraw to make two holes, 5cm (2in) apart, in the space and push a hanging hook into the top behind the cherub. Bake at 145°C (290°F/Gas 1$\frac{1}{2}$) for 2$\frac{1}{2}$ hours.

Painting and Finishing

● Mix up some flesh colour and paint all the cherub apart from his wings and hair. While still wet, mix a spot of Cadmium Red with watery white and blend this into his cheeks, fingers and toes, running a little into the line of his mouth. Paint his wings white and then add a touch of Ultramarine to make a pale blue. Blend this colour into the ends of his wings and also use it to paint his eyes. When his wings are quite dry, tip their very ends with Gold and use the same colour to paint his hair.

Add a little Fir Green to watery Burnt Umber to paint the holly branch and leave to dry. Paint each bunch of leaves separately using pure Fir Green, with Lemon Yellow blended along the edges of each leaf. Use pure Spectrum Red to paint the berries.

Paint the flowers white and work on only two or three at a time to blend a mixture of Lemon Yellow and a touch of Fir Green into their centres and onto their stamens before the white dries. Mix a little Raw Umber into some white to paint the robin's head, back and wings. When this is dry, paint his chest and under his chin with Spectrum Red. Take some fairly fluid Raw Umber onto a fine brush and paint a stylized feather pattern on his back, tail and wings; add a dot of the same colour to his eyes. I have also decorated his feathers with little dots of Gold. Varnish the wreath. When dry thread some wide red ribbon through the holes in the bottom and tie a bow.

Christmas Wreath

· NATIVITY SCENE ·

It is worth taking trouble with this project which could well become a family heirloom. Although it will spend most of its time packed away in a box along with other Christmas decorations, once a year its moment will come — and who knows how many generations will admire your artistry or even try to emulate it when the paint begins to fade?

1¼ quantities Basic Dough, see page 6
plastic ruler
clay gun or garlic press
retracted ballpoint pen
5cm (2in) round fluted cutter
modelling tool • kitchen foil
fine sieve • medium daisy cutter
2 Hanging Hooks, see page 11
Egg Glaze, see page 7
rigger brush

1   Take a handful of dough and make a 20cm (8in) long, finger-thick rope, see page 8. Lay this on a baking try. Make two more ropes about twice as thick and 15cm (6in) long. Score these lengthways with the side of a ruler to represent columns, then stand one at each end of the first rope and secure with a little water. Make a rope similar to the first and lay it across the top of the columns. To shape the roof, roll one more finger-thick rope, about 25cm (10in) long, and fix its ends to the ends of the rope across the top of the columns. Curve the rope upwards so that it forms a domed roof.

2   Pass dough through a clay gun or garlic press to make short lengths of thatching for the roof. Gradually build up a thatch to cover the domed rope and fill the roof space, also cover the rope across the bottom of the roof.

3   To make the back of Mary's chair, if you are using a clay gun, fit the disc that resembles a clover leaf and twist the dough as it comes through. Cut two 5cm (2in) lengths of the twist and lay them about 2.5cm (1in) apart in the middle of the stable. Place a tiny ball of dough on each. If you are not using a clay gun, make two small ropes with a ball on each.

4   Model a small figure with a long skirt but no petticoat, see Carol Singers, page 29. Make the head but do not mark the eyes and mouth, just model a small nose. Make a very thin rope of dough for the neckline of the dress and indent it with a retractable ballpoint pen. Use the same method to decorate the hem of the dress.

5   When the figure is dressed, bend the legs into a sitting position and secure her so that she looks as though she is on the chair. Make a small oval of dough for the baby's body and attach a little ball of dough at one end for the head. Add a tiny nose and wrap the baby in a shawl made by cutting out a circle of rolled-out dough with the fluted cutter. Mark a faint pattern on the shawl with the pointed end of a modelling tool. Arrange the baby in Mary's arms and attach some hair made by extruding dough through a clay gun.

6   Cut a long strip of thinly rolled dough measuring 17.5 × 6.5cm (7 × 2½in). Mark the middle and use this point as a guide for cutting a curve along one side. The strip should still be 6.5cm (2½in) wide at the ends, but the curve should taper its width to only 4cm (1½in) in the middle. Drape this strip over Mary's head, making folds in the ends.

7   Make legs, arms and a body for Joseph, see page 9. Set the arms aside. Cut a triangle from thinly rolled dough, measuring 9cm (3½in) across the base and 12.5cm (5in) along the sides. Cut 12mm (½in) off the apex of the triangle to shape the neck of the robe. Fit the

RIGGER BRUSH

I have used a rigger on many occasions in this book and it is absolutely invaluable if you like to be decorative in your painting by adding a few stripes, checks and tartans. This is a completely straight and narrow brush with hairs about 2.5cm (1in) long. You may buy a synthetic rigger without any qualms as it does not necessarily have a point to go blunt. Charge a rigger well with paint and use its complete length to draw straight lines.

Nativity Scene

STRIPES AND CHECKS

Use a rigger brush to make these designs. If you have never used a rigger before, I would practise first on a piece of paper. Make the paint quite runny, but still opaque, and completely cover the long hairs in your brush with it. Wipe the brush on the side of your palette to make sure that all the hairs are lying straight and then draw your lines, using as much of the length of the brush as you can.

dough around Joseph with the cut off top around his neck. Secure Joseph beside Mary, draping any spare dough in his robe.

8 Fix two thin ropes around Joseph's wrists to make cuffs. Fix the arms onto the body, so that one is around Mary and the other rests across Joseph's body. Flatten a thin rope of dough around the neck of Joseph's robe and indent it with a retracted ballpoint pen. Make a round ball of dough for Joseph's head and add a wedge-shaped nose. Use the clay gun to make a beard and hair for Joseph. Shape a slightly droopy moustache on his face.

9 To make the sheep, roll four thin, 4cm (1½in) long ropes and make a little cut in the middle of one end of each. Arrange these in pairs on the stable base, next to Mary. Cover the tops of the legs with a flattened oval of dough for the body, supporting it on a small pad of foil to prevent it falling back on the baking tray. Model a small ball of dough into a slightly pointed sheep's face and rest it on Mary's cloak, looking at the baby. Flatten two very small balls of dough into cupped ears with the rounded end of a modelling tool. Fix these on the sheep.

10 Make dozens of tiny ropes and roll them up into curls. Secure them to cover the top of the sheep's head and all the body. Secure a few more curls together to make a tail.

11 Roll two pencil-thin ropes and make feet at one end, see page 9. Lay these on the thatched roof. Cut out a triangle of rolled-out dough with a 10cm (4in) base and sides. Still keeping the triangle in shape, tuck the sides under and lay it over the legs with the feet protruding to make the angel's robe.

12 Make a round ball of dough for the head and attach it to the pointed end of the robe. Make a trumpet by rolling out a thin 4cm (1½in) rope which is slightly thicker at one end. Widen the thick end into a trumpet

shape with the rounded end of a modelling tool. Secure the thin end of the trumpet against the angel's face and lay the rest along the left-hand column of the stable.

13 Make hands and arms, and attach cuffs made from very small ropes; secure the arms to the robe. Place the hands on the trumpet. Make a nose from a tiny ball of dough and attach it above the trumpet. Make hair from sieved dough, see page 8.

14 To make wings, cut out two triangles from thinly rolled dough, measuring 4cm (1½in) across each base and 5cm (2in) along the sides. Lay these beside each other, base down, then trim off the outside corner of each. Use a sharp knife to cut pointed shapes into the outer edges. Decorate the points with the retracted ballpoint pen. Place the wings on the angel with the straight sides innermost and the tops of the triangles close to the head.

15 Roll out some dough to 6mm (¼in) and use the daisy cutter to make a star. Secure this firmly to the straw overhanging the left-hand side of the roof. Secure a hanging hook into each side of the roof and brush the roof, columns and base with egg glaze. Bake at 145°C (290°F/Gas 1½) for about 3 hours.

Painting and Finishing

● Mix up flesh colour and paint the faces and hands of all the figures, also Joseph's feet, see page 24. Paint Mary with her eyes closed, looking down at the baby. Add a little Red Ochre to white to make the deep pink of Mary's dress. Add white to Ultramarine to mix the colour of her cloak.

Paint Joseph's robe in pure Burnt Sienna and leave to dry. Use a rigger brush to paint on wide stripes with diluted Yellow Ochre. Mix Cadmium Yellow and Ultramarine to make a dull green and paint more stripes.

Make up watery Permanent White and

paint the baby's shawl and angel's robe and wings. While the wings are wet, blend first a little watery Ultramarine, then some thin Cadmium Red into their edges. Paint the sheep's wool with the same watery white, but do not worry too much about getting paint into all the nooks and crannies, as leaving some dough bare will give the coat depth.

Use pure Jet Black to paint shoes on Joseph's feet and the face and legs of the sheep. When the sheep is quite dry, add pale blue eyes and tint the insides of the ears with watery Cadmium Red. Finally, use Gold to paint the star and angel's trumpet, then paint a design along the hem of the robe and the decoration on the wings. Add a few golden highlights on the hair. Trim the edge of Mary's cloak with Gold and paint a circle and dot pattern over the outside.

· CAROL SINGERS ·

This Dickensian-looking group are a good example of the important role painting takes when trying to produce attractive dough models. The project takes some time to model and it would be truly awful to ruin it with a quick coat of the garish colours that are so often associated with dough modelling.

$1\frac{1}{4}$ quantities Basic Dough, see page 6
fine sieve • cocktail stick (toothpick)
5cm (2in) and 2.5cm (1in) round cutter
fine strip cutter
5cm (2in) fluted round cutter
small blossom plunger cutter
garlic press or clay gun
retracted ballpoint pen
3 Hanging Hooks, see page 11

1 Take a handful of dough and roll it into a fat rope, about 17.5cm (7in) long. Lay this on a baking tray. Make two 6.5cm ($2\frac{1}{2}$in) long ropes for legs and shape quite large shoes at their ends, see page 9; put these to one side.
2 Roll out half of the remaining dough to 3mm ($\frac{1}{8}$in) thick. To make the trousers, cut two 6.5 × 5cm ($2\frac{1}{2}$ × 2in) rectangles and wrap them around the legs, securing them with a little water at the back.
3 Make a fairly portly oval of dough for the man's body and fix this on top of the legs. Do not be too concerned about the join as it will not show. Cut out a 6.5cm ($2\frac{1}{2}$in) square of dough and cut this diagonally into two triangles. Wrap one of these triangles around the right-hand side (*his* right side) of the man's chest so that the cut edge runs across him. Overlapping the first triangle slightly, cover his left side in the same way. Before securing this piece, trim off the point of the triangle where it crosses over to shape the coat front.
4 Cut a pear-shaped piece of dough, about 4.5cm ($1\frac{3}{4}$in) across the fattest part and 6.5cm ($2\frac{1}{2}$in) high. Cut a deep notch in the broad end so that it looks a little like a heart shape and fix this upside down on the figure's back to make coat-tails. Eventually, his right-hand coat-tail will not show because of the female figure but make sure that the left tail is pulled slightly to the side so that it will show from the front.
5 Attach the man to the base rope about 2.5cm (1in) from the right side. Cut two small, tapering strips of dough for coat lapels and secure them in place. Make buttons for the front of the coat from four tiny balls of flattened dough.
6 Make a pair of arms and hands, see page 9, and wrap two thin ropes of dough around these to make cuffs. Attach the arms to the body at the shoulders but leave the hands free. Make a small carol sheet out of a thin piece of dough, about 4 × 2.5cm ($1\frac{1}{2}$ × 1in). Roll up one end to make a scroll, then arrange it in the

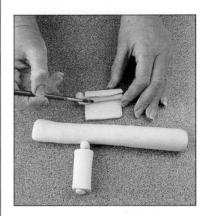

Wrapping the trousers around the legs.

hands so that it looks as if the man is holding it.

7 Make a ball of dough for his head. Mark eyes and an open, singing, mouth with a cocktail stick (toothpick). Make a nose from a small ball of dough. Use the 2.5cm (1in) round cutter to cut out the brim of the hat. Squeeze its edges between your thumb and forefinger to make them thin and to slightly enlarge the brim.

8 Make a short cylinder of dough for the crown of the hat and score it with the back of a knife to make it look slightly battered. Fit the crown on the brim, then put the hat on his head at a slight angle. Push a small amount of dough through the sieve and arrange it in little patches, sticking out from under the hat and on the cheeks to make hair and sideburns.

9 Cut two thin strips of dough 7cm × 12mm ($2\frac{3}{4}$ × $\frac{1}{2}$in). Press the strips gently against the finest strip cutter so that they are indented along their length to look like ribbed knitting. Cross these strips across the man's chest and around his neck to make a scarf. Push some dough through the garlic press to make a fringe for the scarf, see page 8.

10 Make the lady a slightly thinner set of legs and feet, measuring 6.5cm ($2\frac{1}{2}$in) long and lay them on the work surface. Make a far slimmer oval of dough for her body and fix it to her legs. Cut a fluted circle of thinly rolled dough and frill the edges with a cocktail stick (toothpick), see page 10. Remove the centre of the circle with the 2.5cm (1in) round cutter, then cut the remaining frilled ring to make a strip. Fit this around the lady's legs, just above her ankles, to represent the edge of her petticoat.

11 Cut a 16.5 × 5cm ($6\frac{1}{2}$ × 2in) rectangle of thinly rolled out dough and lay it vertically on the surface. Dampen a point in the middle of the top edge of the dough. Fold about 2.5 cm (1in) of dough inwards on each side of the

damp spot, making an inverted pleat. Dust some flour over the top of this pleat to take up any spare moisture and then roll the top 6mm ($\frac{1}{4}$in) of it with a rolling pin to secure it in place. Trim the top edge straight again and trim the side edges of the rectangle at a slant, so that the top is slightly narrower than the bottom.

12 Fit the pleated skirt around the lady's waist and fold the edges underneath her body and petticoat. The bottom of the skirt should cover the top edge of the frill to conceal the fact that there is no petticoat. Arrange the hemline of the skirt so that the petticoat frill shows a little and she looks quite wind blown. There is no need to conceal the top edge of the skirt as it will not show.

13 Make two arms and a scroll of carols and fit these in a similar way to the man's arms. Make the lady a little round head and mark the features as before but give her a smaller nose; do not add the hair and hat yet.

14 Cut a triangle of thinly rolled dough, 10cm (4in) across the base and with 11.5cm ($4\frac{1}{2}$in) sides. Drape this around the lady's shoulders like a shawl. Cross over the front corners of the shawl. Flatten a small oval of dough and attach it where she might have a brooch to hold the shawl in place. Make some thick fringing for the shawl with short lengths of dough from the garlic press.

15 Cut out a 5cm (2in) circle of rolled-out dough and cut it in half. Fit one half over the back of her head to represent the back of her bonnet, then fit the other half so that it overlaps the first slightly and comes forward to form a peak. Shape the second half by pressing the dough lightly between your thumb and forefinger. Decorate the join with a row of small flowers made using a blossom plunger cutter.

16 Attach a few short strands of dough extruding through the garlic press on either

Carol Singers

side of her face to represent ringlets. Cut four very thin strips of dough with the fine strip cutter to make ribbons for her bonnet. Run one strip under her chin, then notch the ends of two more strips. Attach these to the first strip at one side of her face and let the notched ends hang down over her shawl. Make a bow with the third strip, see page 10, and fix this under her chin, over the ribbons.

17 To make the lamp-post make a 15cm (6in) long rope which is quite thick at one end and tapering to become pencil-thin at the other end. Wrap three thin ropes of dough around it at regular intervals by way of decoration. Fix the fatter end to the base to the left of the lady.

18 Lay another thin 2.5cm (1in) long rope across the top of the lamp-post. Stand two more equally thin, 12mm ($\frac{1}{2}$in) long ropes on either end of the first to produce a 'U' shape and top this off with the small, hand-modelled triangle of dough, about 4.5cm ($1\frac{3}{4}$in) across the bottom and 1.5cm ($\frac{3}{4}$in) on each side. Decorate the top of the triangle with two small balls of dough, the top being the smallest. Model a tiny flame and attach it to the middle of the lamp. Then use the retracted ballpoint pen to indent the bottoms of the triangle and the lamp, and the three decorative ropes.

19 Cover the base with several flattened balls of dough, packed tightly together to represent cobble stones.

20 Make two dog's legs by rolling two very thin ropes about 2.5 cm (1in) long. Set these aside for a moment and model a haunch with a leg attached by rolling a 2.5cm (1in) long rope the same thickness as the first pair of legs at one end but growing thicker towards the other end. Flatten the thick end slightly to represent the haunch. Make three short cuts in the bottom of each leg to represent paws.

21 Model an oval of dough for the dog's body and lean this at a slight angle against the male figure's left leg. Fit the two front legs to the front of the body and the haunch and leg to the back, so that the dog appears to be sitting down. Model a smaller oval of dough for the head and fix this onto the dog, tipped up in the direction of the man's face. Mark two eyes and an open mouth with a cocktail stick (toothpick) so that the dog appears to be howling and joining in with the singing. Cut two triangular ears and fit these well back on the dog's head to accentuate the angle of the head. Make a 2.5cm (1in) long tapering rope and fit this on the dog for a tail. Finally, add a small triangular knob of dough just above the mouth for his nose and score the whole dog with your cocktail stick to simulate fur.

22 Push a hanging hook into each end of the base and one into the female figure's hat. Bake at 145°C (290°F/Gas $1\frac{1}{2}$) for about 3 hours.

Painting and Finishing

● Mix some flesh colour, see page 24, and paint the faces of the figures. Use Yellow Ochre to paint the man's trousers and while this is drying paint his jacket with Fir Green. When both jacket and trousers are dry, paint his scarf and gloves in pure Cadmium Red. Then use a fine brush or preferably a rigger and the same colour to paint the red checks on his trousers. When this is dry use some Fir Green to paint a finer check between the red lines, see page 28. Use Jet black to paint the man's lapels, buttons, hat, boots and cuffs.

Paint the lady's shawl in a mixture of white and Ultramarine. While this is drying, paint her skirt pure Magenta and then use the same colour to paint a fine check on her shawl. Allow this to dry thoroughly. Using Ultramarine and white again, mix a slightly darker blue to paint another check between the first lines on the shawl.

Paint the bonnet, ribbons and gloves in pure Spectrum Violet and the flowers on the bonnet with a selection of pale Violets and Magentas, made by mixing white with both these colours.

When the dress is completely dry, paint a triangular pattern all over it in white, using three small dots. While you still have the white on your brush, make it a little more watery and paint both the scrolls and her petticoat and cuffs. When the scrolls are dry, make a few uneven black lines on them to represent writing and paint her boots and the markings on his gloves black.

To finish the lady, paint a miniature portrait on her brooch. Alternatively, paint two or three simple flowers or just paint it black, like ebony.

Paint the dog mainly Burnt Sienna, just dabbing a little white on his chest, tail and paws when the base is dry. Paint his nose and eyes black, putting a little crescent of white at the bottom of his eye when the black is dry, to give the impression that he is looking up. Mix some pink from Cadmium Red and white, and paint the inside of the dog's mouth.

Make up watery Olive Green to paint the lamp post; leave to dry. Paint the balls at the top and the decorative indentations in Gold. If you painted an elaborate brooch, you could also give it a gold frame.

Mix bright orange using Cadmium Red and Yellow for the flame, and add a dab of pure Cadmium Yellow while the paint is still wet.

Mix some white and black together in rather a watery consistency and paint this onto the cobbles. While the paint is still wet, add some watery dabs of blues, violets and pinks to give it some life – but take care not to overdo this effect.

BREAD DOUGH
FESTIVE TABLE
· CENTREPIECE ·

By the time the food has been set on the festive dinner table, there is not very much room for a centrepiece and many of my more extravagant efforts have ended up on the sideboard or — worse still — under it.

hand cream
½ quantity Bread Dough, see page 6
Cadmium Red gouache or water colour paint
waxed paper
large and medium rose leaf cutters
cling film (plastic wrap)
modelling tool
small black stamens
Olive Green gouache or water colour paint
holly leaf cutter
primrose cutter
piece of tree bark, about 20cm (8in) long
gold spray paint
sauce bottle top
fast drying glue
Lemon Yellow gouache or water colour paint
Jet Black gouache or water colour paint
small yellow stamens
Linden Green gouache or water colour paint
spirit-based clear gloss acrylic varnish
candle
50cm (20in) wide green ribbon

1 Rub hand cream into your hands, then take a piece of bread dough about the size of a large walnut, and colour it with Cadmium Red paint, see page 7. Flatten the dough into a round and place it between two pieces of waxed paper, then gently roll it out thinly.

2 Use the larger of the two rose leaf cutters to cut out fourteen poinsettia bracts or petals.

Rolling a modelling tool on a bract to give it a slightly undulating edge.

Gluing the poinsettia bracts onto the bark.

Knead the scraps of dough together and roll them out again; cut out ten more bracts with the smaller rose leaf cutter. Gather up the scraps again and wrap them in cling film.

3 Rub more hand cream onto your hands and on the rounded end of a modelling tool. Lay one of the bracts in the palm of your hand and carefully roll the rounded end of the modelling tool along each side of it to stretch the dough slightly and give the bract slightly undulating edges. Repeat with the remaining bracts and set them aside on a piece of waxed paper to dry.

4 Roll the remaining red dough into eight small balls to represent holly berries. Trim most of the stalk from one of the black stamens and fix it into one berry; repeat with the other berries, then set them aside to dry with the leaves.

5 Take a slightly larger piece of white dough than before and colour it with Olive Green paint, see page 7. Roll this out between waxed paper, then cut out eight leaves with the large rose cutter and seven holly leaves. Roll the edges of the rose leaves as before and set these and the holly leaves aside to dry.

6 Roll out a small piece of the white dough as before and use the primrose cutter to cut out five Christmas roses. Rub more hand cream into your hands and on the rounded end of the modelling tool. Lay a flower in the palm of your hand and gently press and roll each of the petals with the modelling tool before finally pressing it in the middle so that it cups slightly. Repeat with the remaining flowers, then set them aside on waxed paper to dry. Finally, make about twenty very small white balls and leave these to dry.

Painting and Finishing

● Make sure that the piece of bark is clean and dry, and then spray it sparsely with gold paint, so that it receives just a dusting of gold, allowing the wood to show through. Wash and dry the sauce bottle top and give that a solid coat of gold. Leave both until completely dry.

Use fast-drying glue to fix the sauce bottle top upside down on the bark to act as a candle holder.

Paint the poinsettia petals with Cadmium Red and the leaves with a mixture of Olive Green and Lemon Yellow. Allow these to dry before painting some veins on the leaves with pure Olive Green. Paint the holly leaves with pure Olive Green and the holly berries with Cadmium Red. Add a touch of Jet Black to the stamens when the berries are dry.

Paint the Christmas roses white and allow these to dry, then glue four or five yellow stamen heads into the middle of each flower. When the glue has dried, paint some watery Linden Green on and around the stamens, and blend this into the white with a clean damp brush. Finish the stamens by brushing some pure Linden Green over their tops.

Glue seven of the larger poinsettia bracts overlapping each other slightly forming a circle on the bark and with part of the circle leaning up against the candle holder.

Fix five small bracts inside the larger ones so that they overlap in a similar way to form the centre of the flower. Glue ten small balls into the middle of the flower and fix three or four leaves behind the outer bracts.

Make a second arrangement with the remainder of the poinsettia bracts and leaves, and position this so that it also obscures the sides of the candle holder. Fill the centre with the remaining little balls.

Arrange five holly leaves together so that some lean against the candle holder and some lay on the bark. Then position five holly berries in the centre of the group. Lay the remaining holly leaves and berries close to the

Bread Dough Festive Table Centrepiece

Rolling dough between sheets of waxed paper.

Cutting and shaping the Christmas Roses.

second poinsettia and dot the Christmas roses around singly and in pairs to balance the arrangement.

When all the flowers are in place and the glue is dry, give all the dough pieces a coat of spirit-based acrylic varnish and allow this to dry thoroughly.

Finally, fix the candle into the holder and add a bow of green ribbon; glue this at one end of the arrangement close to the candle.

BREAD DOUGH · NAPKIN RINGS ·

If you have decided to revitalize old napkin rings, remember that they do not have to be a matching set; as long as they are similar in size, the gold spray will disguise their appearance.

4 wooden or plastic napkin rings
gold spray
¼ quantity Bread Dough, see page 6
Olive Green gouache or water colour paint
Cadmium Red gouache or water colour paint
waxed paper
medium and very small holly leaf cutter
primrose cutter
yellow and black stamens
P.V.A. glue
spirit-based acrylic varnish
clear fast-drying glue
1.25m (50in) narrow green ribbon

1   Spray the napkin rings gold, giving them several thin coats and leaving the recommended time between applications.

2   Colour about a third of the dough with Olive Green paint, see page 7. Flatten the dough into a circle and then roll it out thinly between two sheets of waxed paper. Cut out eight of each size holly leaf and mark a central vein on each of them. Brush some P.V.A. glue on the backs of two large leaves and lay these on one of the rings, so that they meet end to end and follow the curve of ring. Glue two small leaves in front of the first two at a slight angle. Fix holly leaves on the other rings.

3   Roll out half the remaining dough between waxed paper as before. Use the primrose cutter to cut out eight Christmas roses and shape them with a modelling tool.

4   Take one of the napkin rings and glue two Christmas roses side by side where the larger holly leaves meet. Trim most of the stalks from twelve yellow stamens and push six of them carefully into the centre of each of the flowers. Decorate the other rings similarly.

5   Colour the remaining dough red, see page 7, and roll this into twelve small balls to represent holly berries. Trim most of the stalk from twelve of the black stamens and push one of these into each of the berries. Glue the berries in threes between the flowers and holly leaves. Leave for about 6 hours, until the dough has set and the glue has dried.

Painting and Finishing

● Paint the holly with pure Olive Green and the berries with Cadmium Red. Then paint the Christmas roses white and, before this is quite dry, dab the centres with a little watery Linden Green. When the Christmas roses are completely dry brush some pure Linden Green across the tops of the stamens. Paint the stamens in the berries Jet Black.

Varnish with spirit-based acrylic varnish and allow this to dry thoroughly. Use fast-drying glue to attach a bow of green ribbon tucking it in behind the Christmas roses.

· CHRISTMAS ·
PLACE NAMES

These salt-dough place names do not take much longer to make than a batch of mince pies but, if you pack them away carefully, they will last far longer.

¾ quantity Basic Dough, see page 6
5cm (2in) fluted round cutter
cocktail stick (toothpick)
thin plastic drinking straw
very small holly leaf cutter
Egg Glaze, see page 7
1.5m (62in) narrow red ribbon
fast-drying glue

1 Roll out about a third of the dough to 6mm (¼in) thick and cut out six 6.5 × 12mm (2½ × ½in) strips; set these aside.

2 Roll out some fresh dough to 3mm (⅛in) thick and cut out six fluted circles. Frill the edges of the circles with a cocktail stick (toothpick), see page 10, leaving their centres complete. Cut a third from each frilled circle and set these pieces aside. Use a thin plastic drinking straw to make ribbon eyelet holes at regular intervals about 12mm (½in) in from the frilled edge of the remaining pieces.

3 Lay the large pieces on a baking tray and fix one of the strips, side on, along the unfrilled edge of each of them. Coat these with egg glaze and bake them at 145°C (290°F/Gas 1½) for about 30 minutes or until firm.

4 While the first pieces are baking, make similar eyelet holes in the remaining sections and set them aside with the rest of the dough; cover with a lightly dampened cloth.

5 Stand the baked pieces up so that the frilled part stands up like a shell at the back. Roll six very thin ropes and use these to stick

Christmas Place Names and Christmas Napkin Rings (page 38)

Fixing strips on the unfrilled side of a large piece.

Fixing the smaller frilled section on the baked pieces.

CRAFT TIP

Napkin rings are a law unto themselves and no two ever seem to turn out exactly alike or even, sometimes, precisely as you planned, but it really does not matter, they always look wonderful on the table.

the smaller frilled pieces on top of the front of the strips. Brush the front and the back of the larger frilled pieces with egg glaze.

6 Roll out some dough thinly and cut out twelve very small holly leaves. Arrange these in pairs on the fronts of all the holders and add a few very small balls of dough for berries.

7 Return the holders to the oven, standing them upright, and bake for about 1 hour at the same temperature. If the base of the holder has risen or become slightly puffy during the first baking, lay a metal knife handle across it during the second cooking.

Painting and Finishing

● Paint the holly leaves with pure Olive Green and allow to dry. Then paint the edges of the frills, the holly berries and some lining on the base in Spectrum Red. Varnish in the usual way and allow to dry.

Start threading a piece of ribbon from each end of the back frill on one of the holders. Leave the tails of the ribbon at the back of the holder and thread the pieces of ribbon through the eyelets until they meet in the middle. Tie the ends into a small bow at the front and trim off any excess ribbon. Turn to the back of the holder and trim the ribbon tails, leaving just enough to secure them in place with a dab of fast-drying glue. Finish all the holders in the same way.

These Christmas napkin rings make a charming, rustic addition to the table, particularly if you make matching place names and bowls.

4 cardboard cylinders from kitchen paper or toilet rolls
cooking foil
¾ quantity Basic Dough, see page 6
plastic ruler
5cm (2in) fluted round cutter
cocktail stick (toothpick)
2.5cm (1in) round cutter
small holly leaf cutter
thin plastic drinking straw
Egg Glaze, see page 7
rigger brush
1m (40in) narrow red ribbon
fast-drying glue

1 Cover the cardboard cylinders with cooking foil and set them aside. Roll out half the dough to 6mm (¼in) thick; using a well-floured ruler and a sharp knife cut four 2.5cm (1in) wide strips long enough to fit around the cylinders. Wrap the strips around the cylinders and fix the ends together with a little water. Flour the joins lightly in case they are damp and then stand the cylinders and rings, join downwards, on a baking tray.

2 Roll out some more dough to 3mm (⅛in) thick and cut out four circles with the fluted cutter. Frill the edges of the circles with a cocktail stick (toothpick), see page 10, and then remove the middle of each with the small round cutter to make rings.

3 Cut the rings in half and then fix two halves facing each other, on either side of the top of each napkin ring. If the frills are likely to fall back, prop them up with foil.

4   Cut out twelve holly leaves and arrange these in groups of three on top of each ring, adding a few small balls of dough for berries. Starting on either side of the holly, use a thin drinking straw to make two or three holes around the sides of the rings; these will be used for threading ribbon.

5   Paint the rings, excluding the holly, with egg glaze and bake at 145°C (290°F/Gas 1½) for about 1½ hours.

Painting and Finishing

● Paint all the leaves with Olive Green and leave to dry. Paint the berries and the edge of the frill with Spectrum Red. Use a rigger brush to paint a single red line around each of the rings on either side of the ribbon holes.

Varnish in the usual way; you may like to use yacht varnish as the napkin rings could come into contact with liquid. When the varnish is dry, thread the ribbon through the holes and glue the ends neatly on the inside.

· ROCKING HORSE ·

The following quantity will make two rocking horses. Divide the dough in half before following the instructions.

½ quantity Basic Dough, see page 6
2.5cm (1in) round cutter
retracted ballpoint pen
modelling tool
Hanging Hook, see page 11
30cm (12in) narrow red ribbon

1   Model a handful of dough into a pear shape with a slightly elongated neck. Flatten this slightly and put it to one side. Make three pencil-thin, 5cm (2in) long ropes and trim one end of each at a slant. Use the back of a

knife to indent a line around each rope, about 6mm (¼in) above the trimmed end, to make a hoof.

2   Lay two of the legs on a baking try, with the hooves about 9cm (2½in) apart and the rest of the legs slanting inwards. Wet the tops of the legs and lay the pear-shaped piece on top for the body, so that it overlaps them by about 12mm (½in). The body should be slightly tilted with the neck on your left.

3   Round the end of the third leg opposite the hoof, if necessary, by modelling it with your fingers. Shape the leg into a trotting position and fix it on top of the body so that it lays just ahead of the other front leg. Model the fourth leg in a similar way, but this time make it 6.5cm (2½in) long and allow it to become much wider above the first 3cm (1¼in). Make a hoof at the narrow end and mould the wide end into a round haunch. Secure it to the rear of the body. The leg should lay in front of the other back leg.

Bending and attaching the trotting leg.

Walking Stick

The bright walking stick is made from red, green and white ropes of Bread Dough, see page 6, twisted together and curved into the shape of the handle. Add a hanging hook at the top. When dry, the dough is given an additional coat of paint before being varnished. Gold cord and a double bow of red ribbon decorate the walking stick which is ready to hang on the Christmas tree.

4 Roll a 15cm (6in) pencil-thin rope and flatten it with your fingers before curving it under the hooves of the horse, so that three of them touch it. Fix the three legs to the rocker with a little water. Decorate it around the edge with the retracted ballpoint pen.

5 Model a small piece of dough into an oval for the head. Indent across the top of the narrower end with the back of a knife to mark the mouth. Secure the head on the body. Use the pointed end of one of your modelling tools to mark two nostrils and a slight indentation at either end of the mouth.

6 Flatten two very small balls of dough and secure these on the face as eyes. Indent them horizontally across the middle, with the back of a knife. Use the 2.5cm (1in) round cutter to cut a circle of thinly rolled dough and divide it into four wedges. Round the points on two wedges slightly to make ears.

7 Roll a very thin rope of dough about 4cm (1½in) long and fix it across the horse's face as a nose band. Make an indented pattern on the nose band with the pointed end of a modelling tool and make a tiny ring of dough to go at one end of it. Use the 2.5cm (1in) cutter to cut out a circle of rolled-out dough and cut it in half. Take one of the semi-circles and thin and enlarge it slightly between your fingers and thumb. Place this on the horse's back as a saddle and indent the edges of it with the retracted ballpoint pen. Cut a thin strip of dough about 4cm (1½in) long; secure it from the saddle under the horse's stomach.

8 Roll several long, thin and tapering ropes for the horse's tail and secure these in place in a bunch. Make similar, but shorter, ropes for the mane and attach them along the neck and between his ears. Finally, roll a very thin rope for reins and loop this through the ring on the nose band and over the horse's back. Put a

hanging hook in the top of the saddle. Bake at 145°C (290°F/Gas 1½) for about 1 hour.

Painting and Finishing

● Make up watery grey by adding black to Permanent White and paint the horse. While this is still wet, mix pale pink from white and a touch of Flame Red, add it to the muzzle and blend it into the rest of his face. Add a little more black to the grey and paint uneven patches across the top of his back and legs.

Use pure white to paint the lower half of his eyes and dry. Use black to make a dot in the centre of the white and to run along the eyelid edge. Use black on the hooves and reins.

Paint the nose band, saddle and girth in Flame Red and the rocker in Fir Green. When dry, paint on Gold decoration. Use the gold to paint a wavy line down the middle of the rocker and to paint the nose band ring.

Varnish and dry. Loop half the ribbon through the hanging hook and knot the ends together. Let the knotted end hang down behind the horse and tie a bow around the base of the looped ribbon, close to the top of the hook.

CHRISTMAS · STOCKINGS ·

½ quantity Basic Dough, see page 6
round-ended modelling tool
plastic drinking straw
garlic press or clay gun
cocktail stick (toothpick)
30cm (12in) narrow red ribbon
15cm (6in) narrow gold card
fast-drying glue

1 Take a small handful of dough and make a fairly thick rope measuring about 15cm (6in) long. Mould one end into a stocking foot by squaring it off slightly with your fingers, then pulling one corner into more of a point for the toe, while bending it over a little to make an instep.

2 Insert the round-ended modelling tool into the top and push out the sides of the rope until you have widened the top of the stocking to about 10cm (4in) in circumference. Pinch the back of the stocking top and pull it up gently until it is about 2.5cm (1in) higher than the front. Make a hole in the back, quite near the top, with the plastic drinking straw.

3 Put your fingers into the stocking to support it, then make small indentations with the back of a knife around the edge to simulate ribbing. Still keeping your fingers in place, go around the stocking again, making small holes at the base of the ribbing with a cocktail stick (toothpick).

RAG DOLL STOCKING

4 To fill the rag doll stocking, place it on the baking try and mould a little rectangular dough parcel. Place this on end in the back of the stocking and make a ball of dough to go in front of it. Push them both down into the stocking a little so that they hold it open.

5 Make a small oval of dough for the doll's torso and place this in the stocking so that it slightly overlaps the edge, but is down far enough not to need any skirt or legs. Make two very thin 2.5cm (1in) long ropes for the doll's arms and slightly flatten the rounded ends of them to make simple hands. Secure these on the body so that they flop out of the stocking. Then make a small ball of dough for the head. Secure the head at a floppy angle and mark two eyes and a mouth with a cocktail stick (toothpick). Make the nose from a tiny ball of dough and the hair from dough that has been pressed through the garlic press or — better still — extruded through a clay gun. Hair made with a clay gun is finer.

TEDDY BEAR STOCKING

6 First put a small square parcel of dough into the stocking, then add a small ball of dough to represent an orange. Prick the orange lightly all over with a cocktail stick (toothpick).

Make a small oval of dough for the teddy's body and indent a line down the middle with the back of a knife. Put this into the stocking so that it is leaning out.

7 Make a head from a small pear-shaped piece of dough. Fix a tiny ball of dough at the pointed end of the pear shape to represent the teddy's nose, then fix the head on the body. Mark two eyes with a cocktail stick (toothpick) and make two ears by pressing the rounded end of the modelling tool into two small balls of dough. Secure the ears on the head. Then make two thin ropes of dough, about 2cm ($\frac{3}{4}$in) long, for the arms. Attach these so that one is flopping over the side. Model a tennis racket out of a small circle of dough and a thin rope. Stick this, head up, into the back of the stocking.

8 Bake the stockings together at 145°C (290°F/Gas 1$\frac{1}{2}$) for about 1 hour.

Painting and Finishing

RAG DOLL STOCKING

● Paint the stocking white, apart from the toe, heel and ribbing; dry. Starting with the ribbing and using Flame Red, paint three stripes fairly close together around the stocking. Continue to paint red stripes, keeping them further apart on leg and foot. Paint the heel and toe solid red. When dry, paint alternate stripes in Fir Green. The ribbed section is red and green, the rest is red, white and green.

Mix up flesh colour, see page 24, and paint the doll's face and about three quarters of her arms. Paint her body and short sleeves in pure

Christmas Tree

A Christmas tree cutter was used to stamp out the hanging decoration in Basic Dough, see page 6. Once the parcels, decorations and a hanging hook were fixed in place the tree was baked for about 1 hour. When painted and varnished, gold cord was used to complete the decoration.

Father Christmas

Cadmium Yellow. When dry, paint white spots and cuffs on her dress.

Divide the ball up into eight sections. Using Saffron Green, Ultramarine, orange made from Cadmium Red and Cadmium Yellow, and pale blue made from Ultramarine and white, paint pairs of opposite sections in the same colour. Paint a dot of Flame Red where all the sections meet. Finally, paint the oblong box in pure Rose Pink.

TEDDY BEAR STOCKING

● Paint the stocking Flame Red and dry. Paint a stripe around the ribbing, the toe and heel in pure white. Paint the square box Saffron Green and the orange by mixing Cadmium Red and Yellow. Use Yellow Ochre to paint the teddy and the middle of the tennis racket; dry. Paint Jet Black strings. Paint a small black cross in the middle of the orange. Paint the bear's nose, eyes and claws black. Paint the handle and frame of the racket in Fir Green. Varnish and dry. Thread half the ribbon through each hole and tie the ends in a bow in front of the hole. Add a dab of glue to secure the bow.

Glue gold cord and bows on the boxes.

Christmas Tree

The materials will make two decorations. Divide the dough in half before starting.

¾ quantity Basic Dough, see page 6
cocktail stick (toothpick)
garlic press
Hanging Hook, see page 11
30cm (12in) very thin gold cord
fast-drying glue

1 Take a small handful of the dough, divide it in half and roll two 9cm (3⅜in) long, tapering ropes. These should be finger thick at one end and slightly less than pencil-thin at the other end. Trim the thicker ends at a slant. Secure a thin rope around the thinner end of each, about 2.5cm (1in) from the end. Secure the slanting ends together with a little water and place them on a baking tray.

2 Mould another small handful of dough into a fairly thick circle, measuring about 5cm (2in) across for the body. Place this over the legs so that it overlaps them by about 2.5cm (1in) and secure with a little water.

3 Make a pencil-thin 10cm (4in) long rope of dough and secure it around the lower edge of the circular body so that it will eventually look like fur trimming on a jacket. Make two 7.5cm (3in) long arms with hands, see page 9, and attach a thin rope around the wrist of each of these. Trim the tops of the arms at a slant and secure them to the body with a little water. Model two parcel shapes, one square and one oblong, and secure the arms and hands around these in a carrying position.

4 Secure a round ball of dough on top of the body for the head. Mark two eyes and a mouth with a cocktail stick (toothpick). Make a slightly larger than usual nose from a small ball of dough and add two small, flattened balls of dough for cheeks, see page 44. Fix two tapering wedge shapes underneath the nose to represent a moustache and indent this with the back of a knife to suggest hair. Make a beard and some hair from dough which has been passed through a garlic press.

5   Roll out a small amount of dough to 3mm ($\frac{1}{8}$in) thick and cut out a triangle with a 7.5cm (3in) base and sides. Turn two of the sides under slightly, then fit the base across the front of the head, just above the eyes, to make a hat. Bend the point over slightly and secure one ball of dough on the end of the hat and a second in the middle. Fix a thin 7.5cm (3in) rope around the edge of the hat as trimming.

6   Put two small, flattened balls of dough on his coat between the end of his beard and the fur trimming to make some buttons. Make two little holes in each of these with a cocktail stick (toothpick).

7   To finish, flick the point of the cocktail stick all over the ropes around his legs, arms, hat and coat to simulate fur. Treat the two bobbles on his hat in the same way. Put a hanging hook in the top of his hat and bake at 145°C (290°F/Gas 1$\frac{1}{2}$) for about 1 hour.

Painting and Finishing

● Mix up some flesh colour, see page 24, and paint his face and hands. Paint the suit and hat with Flame Red. When dry, paint the fur trimming white and the boots Jet Black.

Paint one parcel Olive Green and the other Rose Pink and dry. Paint white dots all over the pink parcel. When dry, encircle the dots with Gold. Paint Gold Christmas trees on the green parcels and gold buttons on his coat. Finish the green parcels by painting little red dots between the trees.

Varnish and dry. Glue lengths of cord around the parcels. Dry before gluing bows on each parcel. Tie a bow through the hanging hook.

Christmas Tree Angel

BREAD DOUGH CHRISTMAS ·TREE ANGEL·

about $\frac{1}{3}$ quantity Bread Dough, see page 6
waxed paper
cocktail sticks (toothpicks)
P.V.A. glue
modelling tool
Hanging Hook, see page 11
piece of polystyrene
retracted ballpoint pen
garlic press

1   Take a small piece of the dough and roll two thin ropes each about 5cm (2in) long. Flatten one end of both of them slightly and

CRAFT TIP

Unlike salt dough figures, bread dough people have to be made up of separate pieces which are assembled only when dry. This means that they take a lot longer to make and that care has to be taken over the proportions of all the parts.

43

Gluing the legs into the gown.

Moulding the cheeks onto the face.

make a pair of feet, see page 9. Make some thin arms and hands, about 4cm (1½in) long, see page 9, and put these and the legs to dry on a piece of waxed paper.

2   Roll a small ball of dough for the head. Mark the eyes and a small hole for the mouth with a cocktail stick (toothpick). Make a tiny ball of dough for the nose and glue this in place. Place the head on a cocktail stick and stand it in a piece of polystyrene until it dries.

3   To make the trumpet, roll a tapering rope about 2.5 cm (1in) long. Open up the broad end by inserting a modelling tool and then roll this until the dough is hollowed and widened into a trumpet shape. Put this to one side to dry.

4   Roll out another small piece of dough thinly between two sheets of waxed paper. Cut out two triangles with equal sides of 3cm (1¼in) each. Cut three fairly deep notches in one side of each triangle to make wings, and then indent a pattern on these feathery pieces with the retracted pen.

5   When the legs are dry, take a small ball of dough and flatten it out into a circle large enough to make the angel's gown. Indent the edge of the circle with the ballpoint pen and then curve and glue it into a cone. Glue the legs inside the gown so that the front of the feet show beneath the edge of the dough on the side without the join. Push a short hanging hook into the back of the gown.

6   Use smaller circles of dough to make sleeves in a similar way to the gown. Then lay all these pieces to dry on waxed paper.

7   When the head is dry, flatten two very small balls and glue them onto the face as puffed-out cheeks. Thin the edges of the cheeks and mould them onto the face.

8   Keep the head fixed into the polystyrene on the end of the cocktail stick (toothpick), while you gradually glue on strands of dough from a garlic press to build up hair.

9   Glue the thin end of the trumpet into the mouth of the angel and support the other end on crumpled paper until the glue has dried.

10   When dry, glue the head onto the point of the cone-shaped gown and attach the tops of the arms on each side of it, so that they are stretched out in the same direction as the trumpet. Glue the hands to the trumpet. Attach the wings to the angel's back and dry.

Painting and Finishing

●   Mix up flesh colour, see page 24 and paint the angel's arms, legs and face. Add a little more Cadmium Red to the mixture and blend this into the cheeks, fingertips and toes.

Paint the gown and wings white. Add a little Ultramarine to make pale blue. Blend this into the ends of the wings while they are damp. Make pink by mixing white and Alizarin Crimson, then blend this into the pale blue wing tips. Use pale blue to paint the angel's eyes. Paint the decoration on the gown and wings, trumpet and hair with gold.

Varnish with spirit-based acrylic varnish or oil-based clear gloss polyurethane varnish.

cover the gold with this colour. While damp blend a mixture of white and Viridian into some areas: mainly in the nooks and crannies around the pots, and between the leaves and grapes, but do not overdo this. When the paint is almost dry, take a soft, lint-free cloth and rub some of it away to reveal the gold. This will look most authentic if you rub back some of the decorative raised areas. Do not rub back so far as to show the dough.

When you are satisfied with the effect, allow the paint to dry and add a coat of clear gloss polyurethane varnish. The gold will gleam if you apply two or three coats of varnish; remember to leave 24 hours between applications.

Shave the bottoms off the little candles and arrange them in the holders.

Candelabra

HIGH DAYS AND HOLIDAYS

Many of the traditional celebrations connected with our high days and holidays have become slightly inappropriate. Since the ancient rituals were mainly pagan in origin, and involved the killing of oxen and dancing naked around bonfires, it is probably just as well that our modern-day festivities are based on more recent history

I know that making dough models by way of celebration might seem comparatively tame to some, but there are some fascinating legends that you might like to link with your pieces of dough. Take the Valentine's day mirror for example, and save it until Halloween. Then, on the stroke of midnight, stare into it, while you simultaneously eat an apple and brush your hair. Providing that you are single, legend has it that your future husband or wife will appear by your side as you take the last bite!

· CHERUBS AND HEARTS ·

It was the Victorians who really made a great romantic festival out of Saint Valentine's day and, as usual, they didn't hold back.

Victorian Valentine cards showed cherubs carrying baskets full of quivering red hearts or staggering under overflowing cornucopias of them, while others were often depicted understandably exhausted and asleep on huge piles of broken hearts. Some cherubs had an easier time of it admittedly and were simply put in charge of flocks of doves or writing and delivering love letters, but that still left the gathering of roses, lace and butterflies to worry about February 14th was a hectic time for the poor old Victorian cherub.

¾ quantity Basic Dough, see page 6
modelling tool
cocktail stick (toothpick)
5cm (2in) heart cutter
1cm (½in) and 2.5cm (1in) round cutters
small and medium blossom plunger cutters
retracted ballpoint pen
2 Hanging Hooks, see page 11

1   For the legs, roll a little of the dough into two pencil-thin ropes, each about 6cm (2½in) long. Lay these side by side and trim their ends at a slant: cut the bottoms of the strips so that their longest sides are together; cut the tops so that the shortest sides are together. Make four short cuts in the bottom of each rope to represent toes. Fix the slanting ends at the tops of the ropes together with a little water.
2   Model a small handful of dough into an egg-shaped body. Dampen the back of this and press it, broadest-end down, on the joined tops of the legs. Flatten two very small balls of dough and fix them on the legs to represent knees. Smooth the edges of the dough into the legs using a damp brush.
3   Roll a suitably sized ball of dough for the

head and fit it onto the body. Then roll a tiny ball of dough for a nose and fix it in place.

4 Use a modelling tool to make a wide smiling mouth and give the cherub some cheeks by flattening two small balls of dough on either side of the mouth, smoothing the dough in place as when making the knees. Mark the eyes with a cocktail stick.

5 Make a left arm and a hand to fit the cherub, see page 9, and fix them onto the body, bending the hand above the head. Make the second cherub in the same way, this time giving him a right hand and arm.

6 Roll out some dough to 6mm ($\frac{1}{4}$in) thick

and cut out two hearts. Overlap these slightly, fixing them with a little water.

7 Roll out some more dough to 3mm ($\frac{1}{8}$in) thick. Use the larger round cutter to make about fourteen rosebuds, see page 11. Arrange the rosebuds at intervals around the edges of the hearts. Use the small blossom plunger cutter to make small blossoms and attach these between the rosebuds.

8 Shape the letters of your choice from very thin ropes of dough and fix them in the middle of the hearts. Decorate them with a retracted ballpoint pen. Arrange the two cherubs, pressed up against the two hearts and leaning in slightly, with their arms on the outside.

Cherubs and Hearts

Using dough to make a frame for a mirror does not have to be restricted to Valentine's day. This design can easily be adapted for Christmas by changing the doves to robins, the heart to a bow and the flowers to holly or Christmas roses. If you are feeling more adventurous, you could change the shape completely and decorate it with just about anything. I often make nautical frames, with seashells, mermaids and fishes. It is actually possible to bake the mirror into the dough (as for the china beads on the Engagement Bowl, see page 63) but as it must never be placed directly on a baking tray and will crack unless it is evenly supported on a bed of dough, it is far safer to glue the mirror on after the frame is baked.

9   Cut out a 25cm (10in) strip of dough. Cut both ends to resemble ribbon. Drape this over the cherubs' heads and bodies, making sure that it passes through their hands. Cut a similar strip of dough and make a bow with tails, see page 10. Fix the bow on the ribbon between the two cherubs' heads, so that the tails drape over the hearts.

10   Model six rosebuds using the smaller round cutter and attach these diagonally across the cherubs' tummies. Use the medium blossom plunger cutter to make flowers to fill in the gaps and add little balls of dough pricked with a cocktail stick.

11   Fix two short, narrow strips at the ends of each garland to represent ribbons. Arrange some fine, rolled up ropes of dough on the cherubs' heads to represent curls. Push a hanging hook into the head of each and bake at 145°C (290°F/Gas 1½) for about 1½ hours.

Painting and Finishing

● Float a very thin Rose Pink wash onto the cherubs' cheeks, tummies, knees, fingertips and toes. Mix some Ultramarine and white to a pale blue and paint the initials, blossoms, long ribbon and bow. Quickly mix some white and Rose Pink, and dab a little pale pink onto the blossoms before the blue is completely dry. Paint the garland roses and ribbons pale pink. Then use pure Rose Pink to paint the roses on the hearts and inside the cherubs' mouths.

When the forget-me-knot blossoms and initials are dry, paint each flower centre with a dab of Lemon Yellow and paint the ballpoint indentations on the initials Gold. Continue to use the Gold on the hair and the edges of the ribbon. Add a little pale blue to the eyes.

Paint the tiny circular flowers on the garland white. Add a little white to Olive Green and paint a few leaves on the garland.

VALENTINE'S DAY
· MIRROR ·

¾ quantity Basic Dough, see page 6
15cm (6in) saucer
10cm (4in) and 2.5cm (1in) round cutters
5cm (2in) fluted round cutter
cocktail stick (toothpick)
large heart crimper
medium rose leaf cutter
primrose cutter
Hanging Hook, see page 11
2–3 stamens
12.5cm (5in) square mirror tile or small mirror
strong glue or hot glue gun

1   Roll out half the dough to 6mm (¼in) thick. Using the saucer as a guide, cut a circle from the rolled-out dough, then use the 10cm (4in) cutter to cut out the middle of the circle. Place the ring of dough on a baking tray.

2   Roll out some more dough to 3mm (⅛in) thick. Cut out about 22 fluted circles with the 5cm (2in) cutter. Then frill the edges of each circle, page 10, repeatedly flouring the cocktail stick. Cut the circles in half and attach about eleven halves to the outside of the large ring so that the frilled curves form a scalloped edge around the outside. Attach the remaining semi-circles in a ring on top of and just inside the first ones. Arrange the second row so that the scallops alternate with the first set.

3   Make a 45cm (18in) long pencil-thick rope of dough. Press this around the dampened inside edge of the upper frill so that it is slightly flattened and then use the crimper to decorate the rope of dough with hearts.

4   Model a plump heart from a walnut-sized piece of dough, making the notch at the top with the back of a knife. Fix this onto the heart

Valentine's Day Mirror

Putting on the first row of frilled semi-circles.

Decorating the inner rim with hearts.

CRAFT TIP

Remember always to paint and varnish the back of any part of a design that overlaps the middle of a mirror as it will be reflected in the glass.

---

border at the top of the mirror frame. Model two doves, see page 11, and arrange them slightly to the right of the heart.

5 Using the rose leaf cutter, cut out and vein seven leaves, see page 11. Place six leaves, in two groups of three, opposite the doves and at the bottom of the frame. Fit the last leaf in between the heart and the doves.

6 Use the 2.5cm (1in) circular cutter to make one large and three smaller roses, see page 11. Place one small rose on the single leaf and the other two side-by-side on the three leaves on the side of the frame. Fix the large rose in the middle of the three leaves at the bottom of the frame. Using the same cutter, make four rose-buds, see page 11, and tuck one of these behind the two small roses. Arrange the other three rosebuds around the single large rose.

7 Cut out three dog roses with the primrose cutter and slightly cup the petals, see page 11. Place two of these close to the doves and the other one near the heart. Arrange three shor-tened stamens in the centre of each dog-rose.

8 Roll two very thin, short ropes of dough and make these into rings to represent wedding rings. Overlap the rings between the doves.

9 Decorate the space between the objects and below the border with dozens of little balls of dough in a variety of sizes, all pierced with the sharp end of a modelling tool. Push a hanging hook behind the lace and the large heart; because this is a heavy item use a whole hook. Bake at 145°C (290°F/Gas 1½) for about 2 hours.

Painting and Finishing

● Dampen the frill around the edge of the mirror with a clean brush dipped in water, then paint on some slightly diluted Permanent White. The white paint on the frill should be opaque but not thick.

Paint the doves and the dog roses with the same mixture, then blush them with a little watery Rose Madder on the petal edges and also on the fronts, tails and the wings of the doves. Use well-diluted Ultramarine to tip the doves' tails and wings.

Paint each of the small hearts on the border with the thin Rose Madder. Paint the leaves with some thin Olive Green and variegate them slightly with some of the thin Rose Madder.

Thicken the Rose Madder by adding some fresh paint and use this to paint the roses, rosebuds and the big heart. Mark the doves' eyes with little specks of Ultramarine. Paint their beaks and the dog rose stamens with an orange, made by mixing Rose Madder and Lemon Yellow.

Trim the edges of the frills, the doves' wings and their tails with some slightly diluted gold paint. Paint the wedding rings gold.

Finally, I have worked a little diluted gold into the tips and around the edges of the leaves to give a more Victorian look — make sure that you leave it at that . . . it is easy to run amuck when armed with gold on a brush and end up with a very garish model!

When the paint is dry, varnish the dough in the usual way, applying a couple of coats to the back. This is to ensure that the dough does not absorb the glue and prevent the mirror from bonding to it. When the varnish is completely dry, fix the mirror to the back of the frame using strong glue. If you use a hot glue gun, place the glue on the back of the frame and allow it to cool for a few seconds before attaching the mirror.

MOTHER'S DAY
· FLOWERS ·

Maybe you should make this the first thing you attempt from the book, after all, you are almost guaranteed an appreciative reception, no matter how 'artistically threatened' the result may be.

1 quantity Basic Dough, see page 6
leaf cutter
medium blossom plunger cutter
cocktail stick (toothpick)
Hanging Hook, see page 11

1   Cut out the jug template, see page 79. Roll out half the dough to 6mm ($\frac{1}{4}$in) thick. Flour the jug template well and gently press it into the dough so that it just makes an indentation. If you feel confident enough to do so, remove the template and cut around the indentation with a sharp knife. Otherwise simply cut around the template.

2   Place the dough jug on a baking tray. Make a finger-thick rope of dough about 17.5cm (7in) long. Coil one end of the rope slightly and fix it about one third of the way up the right-hand side of the jug. Curve the rest of the rope to resemble a handle and fix the end towards the top of the jug. Cut out the tulip leaf template, see page 79.

3   Roll out some more dough to 3mm ($\frac{1}{8}$in) thick. Flouring the tulip leaf template frequently, cut out five leaves. Mark a central vein on each of these with the back of your knife, then arrange them on and around the jug so that all their ends tuck behind it. Fix these in place with a little water.

4   Make five thin ropes of dough in various lengths to represent tulip stems and fix them on and around the jug as for the leaves.

Mother's Day Flowers

5   Cut out the tulip petal template. Using the thinly rolled-out dough, cut out 20 petals in the same way as the jug. Build these up into flower shapes on the end of the stems, laying one petal flat at the back, two curved petals on either side and the last one on the top. Pinch the petals into the stems slightly and fix them in place with a little water.

6   Roll out five more thin stems and arrange them among the tulips for the lilacs. Cut out nine small leaves using the cutter and mark their central veins before arranging them along the lilac stems. Cut out dozens of tiny

Building up the tulip flowers.

---

blossoms from some thinly rolled dough for the lilac sprays. Bake at 145°C (290°F/Gas 1½) for about 2½ hours.

Painting and Finishing

● Add the smallest amount of Lemon Yellow to Olive Green and use to paint the tulip leaves. Add a little more Lemon Yellow and some white to the mixture, then paint the tulip stems and the lilac leaves. Allow the lilac leaves to dry. Using a very fine brush and some pure Olive Green, paint the central vein and some side veins on the lilac leaves.

Mix Cadmium Yellow and Cadmium Red to make a warm orange, and use to paint three of the tulips. While the paint is still wet streak the tulips from top to bottom with pure Cadmium Red, Cadmium Yellow and even a little Lemon Yellow. Blend these colours in slightly with a clean damp brush.

Paint the remaining tulips in pure Cadmium Yellow and treat them in the same way, streaking them with some of the orange mixture, Lemon Yellow and even a little of the pale green mixture near the stems.

Use pure Spectrum Violet to paint two of the sprays of lilac and when these are complete, but still damp, add a little white and a speck of Ultramarine to the paint. Run this over some of the top flowers with a dry brush to give a little variety to the colour.

Add a touch more Ultramarine and some more white to paint the paler lilacs; when they are painted, add more white and run over the top flowers again as you did before.

Paint the jug with a mixture of Ultramarine and white and leave to dry. Paint on a few simple flowers using a similar orange to that on the tulips. Use the same colour to paint a flourish on the handle.

Finally, give the flowers Olive Green middles, stems and leaves; then fill in gaps with large white spots.

· HALLOWEEN WITCH ·

If your family is like mine and never actually manages to achieve any of the idyllic stuff connected with seasonal festivities, but tends to go straight for the foul fiends, you might like to spend halloween making this wicked little witch and her jet-lagged cat.

¾ quantity Basic Dough, see page 6
garlic press or clay gun, or both if possible
plastic ruler
cocktail stick (toothpick)
modelling tool
5cm (2in) and 12mm (½in) round cutters
2 Hanging Hooks, see page 11

1 Roll out a finger-thick rope of dough 22.5cm (9in) long. Place this on a baking tray at a slight angle and score it lightly with a knife to represent bark.

2 If you have a clay gun it is better to use it for the twigs of the broom instead of a garlic press. It is easier to extrude long strands and it gives the dough a better texture. I have used the gun for the twigs and the garlic press for the hair to accentuate the difference. Build up 10cm (4in) lengths of dough from the clay gun over the right-hand end of the broom handle to make a thick bunch of twigs. Dent the twigs slightly about 6mm (¼in) from the end of the broom handle and lay several very thin ropes of dough over the dent to represent binding.

3 Make two 12.5cm (5in) pencil-thin ropes of dough for legs, tapering one end of each to a point. Flatten 2.5cm (1in) of the pointed ends with your finger to make feet. Roll two very thin 2.5cm (1in) ropes of dough and wrap them around the legs just above the feet to look like boot tops. Arrange the legs, one under, and the other over, the broomstick,

Halloween Witch

Gift Tags

*Beautiful gift tags can be made using
the techniques explained in the open-
ing chapter. These are made using
Basic Dough, see page 6.*

then fix them with a little water.

4   Model an oval of dough for the body and
attach it to the broomstick so that it appears to
be leaning forward slightly. Then take half the
remaining dough and roll it out to about 3mm
($\frac{1}{8}$in) thick. Using a well-floured ruler and a
sharp knife, cut out a triangle measuring
17.5cm (7in) across the base and 10cm (4in)
high. Trim 12mm ($\frac{1}{2}$in) from the apex of the
triangle, then drape it around the witch's body
like a dress, fitting the blunted apex around
the neck and tucking the sides under.

5   Roll out two thin ropes for arms making
hands at one end of them and trimming the
other ends at a slant, see page 9. Fit the
slanting ends to the body and rest the hands
on the broomstick.

6   Cut a triangle for the cloak, making it
15cm (6in) across the base and 10cm (4in)
high. Trim 12mm ($\frac{1}{2}$in) from the apex of the
triangle as before, then drape it over the back
of the witch so that it covers the join where the
front arm meets the body. The cloak should
appear to billow out behind the witch. Fold
back the nearest edge of the cloak and cut two
thin strips of dough to use as ties at the front.
Arrange these to look knotted.

7   Fit a ball of dough on the shoulders to
represent the head and model a grinning
mouth with a modelling tool. Fit a tiny ball
of dough into the mouth for the one, and only,
tooth and make a wedge-shaped piece of
dough into a nose. Use a cocktail stick (toothpick) to make two small, close-set eyes. Press
dough through a garlic press to make hair, see
page 8, and arrange it flying back.

8   Cut out a 5cm (2in) circle of dough and
place it on the witch's head for the brim of her
hat. To make the top of the hat, cut a triangle
of rolled-out dough measuring 7.5cm (3in)
across the base and 5cm (2in) high. Bend
this into a conical shape, joining the edges
with a little water. Fit the cone of dough on

top of the brim with the join at the back and
add a narrow strip of dough for a hat band.

9   Model a small oval of dough for the cat's
body and sit this up behind the witch. Roll two
short thin ropes of dough for the cat's legs,
making the back one slightly thicker at one
end to represent his haunch. Cut three little
toes at the paw ends and fix the legs in place on
the body. Make a short, slightly pointed, rope
for the cat's tail and a small ball for his head.

10   Cut a 12mm ($\frac{1}{2}$in) circle of rolled-out
dough and cut it into quarters. Use two of
these quarters for ears and a very small ball
of dough for a nose. Place two very small
flattened balls of dough side by side under
the cat's nose for whisker pads and add a
strip of dough for a collar and a bow, see
page 10.

11   Fix a hanging hook in the twiggy end of
the broom and another in the hat. Bake at
145°C (290°F/Gas 1$\frac{1}{2}$) for about 2$\frac{1}{2}$ hours.

Painting and Finishing

●   Mix up flesh colour and paint the witch's
face and hands, see page 24. As she is
obviously quite a fashion-conscious witch, I
have added a little more Cadmium Red to her
'blusher' and also painted some lipstick and a
beauty spot. Remember to paint her tooth!

Paint the dress, boots, hat band and the
cat's bow in Viridian and allow to dry. Add
golden stars, moons and planets to the dress,
and spots to the hat band and the cat's bow.

Paint the cloak a rich Magenta. Paint the
cat, the witch's stockings and her hat Jet
Black. Finish the cat by adding a little watery
Magenta to the whisker pads, inside the ears
and the paws.

Mix Cadmium Red and Cadmium Yellow
together, adding slightly more yellow. Paint the
witch's mane of red hair. Paint a wash of Raw
Umber on the broom handle and on the binding.

BALLET DANCER · INITIAL ·

Take more than the usual amount of care when making the dough for a rounded initial. It needs to be firm and extremely well kneaded if you are to avoid the dents and cracks that bending such a large amount of dough can cause. However, the nature of salt dough is to look a little rugged and rustic, so there is no need to worry unduly if your models are not always absolutely faultless.

This ballet dancer filled the wide open space of the 'G' quite well, but the continuous curve of the letter looked a little barren until I added the ballet shoes.

¾ quantity Basic Dough, see page 6
15cm (6in) saucer
cocktail stick (toothpick)
garlic press
small blossom plunger cutter
5cm (2in) round fluted cutter
2.5cm (1in) round cutter
1 length medium floristry wire
small leaf cutter
modelling tool
2 Hanging Hooks, see page 11

1   Place the saucer on a baking tray and draw around it with a pencil. Take a little more than half the dough and roll a rope that is about the width of two fingers and about 42.5cm (17in) long. Carefully transfer the rope of dough to the baking tray and curve it around the pencil circle, leaving a gap of about 5cm (2in). Trim the lower end of the open circle, cutting it straight across with a sharp knife.

2   Roll a 5cm (2in) rope of similar thickness and fit it across the trimmed end of the letter with a little water.

3   Roll two thin, 5cm (2in) long ropes for the legs. Make these slightly tapered at one end and trim them diagonally at the other. Attach the tapered ends to the inside of the letter and the slanting ends together for the tops of the legs. Arrange the legs so that the doll will appear to be pirouetting when she is complete.

4   For the body, model a piece of dough about the size and shape of a walnut and fix it, point down, to the top of the legs. Roll out two ropes for the arms. Make these a little shorter and slightly thinner than the legs and model a hand at one end of each, see page 9. Cut the other ends at a slant and fix them in place on the body, placing one hand on the crossbar of the letter and setting the other one out to one side.

5   Cut six 2.5cm (1in) lengths of floristry wire and carefully wrap the free hand around them, fixing them in place with a little water. Roll a small ball of dough for the head. Fix this to the body with a little water and mark two eyes and a mouth with a cocktail stick (toothpick). Attach a tiny ball of dough for the nose. Push some dough through a clay gun or garlic press to make the hair, see page 10, and attach it to the head.

6   Roll out most of the remaining dough to about 3mm (⅛in) thick. Cut out twelve small blossoms to decorate the hair and to make up the posy. Fix these in place with a little water on the wires in the hand and on her head.

7   Using the fluted cutter, cut out three circles of dough and remove the centre of each with the small round cutter. Frill the edges of the rings with a cocktail stick (toothpick), see page 10, then cut and open out one of them so that you have a frilled strip rather than a circle. Attach the curved side of the strip across the body and up at the sides to the arms. Cut a 4cm (1½in) wedge from the

CRAFT TIP

I include two designs for initials, one for a little girl and one for an older gentleman who still fancies himself as a tennis player. The second one is a caricature of someone I know and I am sure that you will have great fun designing similar figures to give to friends.

INITIAL IDEAS

Decorated initials can be made and given to celebrate most personal moments of glory, from birthdays to barmitzvas, the passing of exams to retirements. They are extremely popular and seem to be equally acceptable whether the recipient is young or old, male or female.

Initials are particularly welcome as christening gifts, especially if a little dough scroll or circle is added so that the baby's name and birthday can be printed on it at the painting stage.

second ring. Lay this over the first strip, placing it about 3mm ($\frac{1}{4}$in) higher. Cut a 2.5cm (1in) wedge from the third strip and attach this over the first two in the same way. Lift the frills away from each other slightly to make the skirt look like a tutu and support any rebelliously floppy dough with small pieces of folded cooking foil. Roll a very thin rope of dough and drape this across the chest and around the neck of the figure to create a neckline.

8 Cut out and vein three leaves, see page 11, and place them symmetrically near the cross-bar to cover the join in the dough. Make three roses and two rosebuds, see page 11, and place these in the middle of the leaves.

9 To make the ballet shoes, roll two small ovals of dough and hollow them out slightly with a modelling tool. Attach the ballet shoes to the side of the initial, then decorate them with two tiny bows and four long strips of dough to represent ribbons.

10 Finally, attach two hanging hooks at the top and one at the bottom of the initial. Bake at 145°C (290°F/Gas 1$\frac{1}{2}$) for about 2$\frac{1}{2}$ hours.

Painting and Finishing

● Mix some flesh colour and paint the face and arms, see page 24. Add a little pale blue for the eyes and some red for the mouth.

Brush clean water onto the legs and dress to make them *slightly* damp. Mix a very little Lemon Yellow into watery Permanent White and paint the legs, the two under skirts and the top of the bodice. Add a very little Cadmium Red to the pale yellow and blend this into the colour on the bodice. Complete the bottom of the bodice in this colour and continue it over the waist and about a third of the way down the top layer of the dress. Add a little Cadmium Red to the mixture and blend this into the last colour and a little further down

the skirt. Add a little more red and blend this in a similar way to complete the skirt.

Paint one or two blossoms, a rose, rosebud and shoes with the colour used on the skirt.

Mix some of the other colours used for the dress and paint the posy, garland and remaining roses.

Paint the whole letter with a mixture of white and Ultramarine, making sure that you mix enough paint to complete the whole thing before you start painting. I can guarantee you will never mix exactly the same colour again if you run out!

When the initial has dried paint the leaves Olive Green and add a little Lemon Yellow to this to paint the centres of all the blossoms. Finally, paint the ballet shoes Cadmium Red, adding a little white to complete the linings.

TENNIS PLAYER · INITIAL ·

$\frac{3}{4}$ quantity Basic Dough, see page 6
plastic ruler
cocktail sticks (toothpicks)
garlic press • tweezers
3cm (1$\frac{1}{4}$in) and 2cm ($\frac{3}{4}$in) round cutters
2 lengths fine floristry wire
wire cutters
retracted ballpoint pen
small daisy cutter
modelling tool
butterfly cutter
2 Hanging Hooks, see page 11

1 Using half the dough, roll two ropes each about the width of two fingers. Roll one to about 14cm (5$\frac{1}{2}$in) long and the other to 9cm (3$\frac{1}{2}$in) *without trimming* the dough. This will give the ropes naturally rounded ends, which look more attractive than cut ends. If you have to trim the dough, hold your knife at an angle so that the surface of the rope is slightly proud of its base. Trim a small amount of dough from one end of the longest rope to make a straight edge and attach this to the middle of the shorter rope with a little water to form a 'T'.

2 Roll two fairly thin ropes 7.5cm (3in) long for the legs from a little of the remaining dough. Make sure that at least one end of each rope is rounded. Then form an indentation in each rope, 2cm ($\frac{3}{4}$in) away from the rounded end, by gently rolling your finger across the dough. Dab a little water in these indentations with a brush, then push the rounded end up so that it stands at right angles to the rest of the leg and forms a foot.

3 Roll out half of the remaining dough to about 3mm ($\frac{1}{8}$in) thick. Using a sharp knife and a well-floured ruler, cut two 6.5cm × 3.5cm (2$\frac{1}{2}$ × 1$\frac{1}{2}$in) rectangles. Fit one of these around the top of each leg to represent shorts and secure them at the back with a little water.

4 To make socks, cut another two 5 × 3.5cm (2 × 1$\frac{1}{2}$in) rectangles. Using a cocktail stick (toothpick) roll and pleat the dough so that the pleats are parallel with the longest edges of the rectangles. Leave the top 6mm ($\frac{1}{4}$in) of each piece flat and fold it back before making vertical indentations to represent ribbing. Wrap these around the bottoms of the legs, pushing them well down on the shoes, before securing them at the back with water.

5 Make two very small balls of dough and flatten them slightly before attaching them to the legs, just below the shorts to represent knees. Use a damp brush to smooth the edges of the balls of dough into the legs. Trim the top ends of the legs and shorts diagonally, so that the highest point of the diagonal is on the outside of each.

6 Model a rounded shape for the body. If you want a tall and slim figure, make an oval shape. Pinch the body in slightly at both ends, where the arms and legs are going to fit, then attach the legs with a little water. Dampen the side of the figure slightly and press him against the letter.

7 Roll out two thin ropes of dough for the arms, making sure that they are in proportion to the rest of the body, and make hands at one end, see page 9. Cut a strip of rolled-out dough about 2cm ($\frac{3}{4}$in) deep and 7.5cm (3in) long. Attach this around the top of the left arm to make a sleeve. Trim the top of the sleeve and arm at a slant and attach it to the top of the body so that the arm is raised.

8 Curve a thin strip of dough around the top of the body to represent the neck of the T-shirt. Indicate the ribbing by indenting this with the back of a knife. Make the ribbing at the bottom of the shirt in a similar way.

9 Cut the hand from the second arm and attach it to the other side of the initial, leaving some of the fingers free to hold the string bag. Make the head from a round, smooth piece of dough and mark the eyes and mouth with a cocktail stick (toothpick). Attach a very small ball of dough for the nose. Fit the head in place on top of the body and add a few wisps of garlic-press hair, see page 8.

10 Cut one large and one small circle of rolled-out dough. Press the larger circle out a little between your finger and thumb, then turn in a small hem all around the edge. Cut the smaller circle in half and attach one half to the hemmed side of the larger circle so that it protrudes from underneath like the peak of a cap. Turn the dough over and place it on the model's head.

11 Make seven smooth balls of dough, a suitable size for tennis balls, and pile them up against the far side of the initial, a little way below the hand. Press some dough through

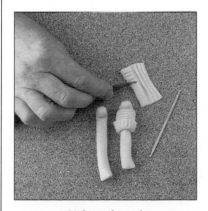

Making the socks.

59

DIFFICULT LETTERS

The letter 'T', like 'L' and 'J', is very suitable for standing figures but it is not so easy to fit in the figure if you are dealing with curved letters, like 'G' and 'Q', or letters with bars, like 'A' and 'H'.

Rounded letters work best with the figure leaning back and curving into the letter, while barred letters look good with the model draped nonchalantly over the crossbar. So you can still decorate initials for the likes of Quentin and Hubert if you take time to make a small preparatory sketch to find the best position for the figure before modelling the dough.

Rogue letters like 'K', 'M' and 'N' take a little more thought than simple letter shapes, but it is always possible to fit the figure in somewhere. Remember that while you do not have to show all the body, you must take care not to obscure the shape of the letter.

the garlic press. Then use well-floured tweezers to lay single strands of dough across the balls to form a string bag. Take some of the vertical strands up beyond the balls and tuck them under the unattached fingers of the hand to form a handle. Secure all the pieces with a little water as you work.

12 To make the tennis racket, roll out a thin rope of dough and form it into an oval to make the racket head. Cut several short lengths of wire and use these to represent the strings of the racket, embedding the ends in the dough frame. Roll a thin rope of dough to represent the handle and attach the head of the racket to it. Place the other end of the handle into the upraised hand of the model. Bring the head of the racket around so that it rests on the top of the initial and attach it with a little water. Roll out another thin rope of dough and lay it on top of the frame as decoration, marking it with a retracted ballpoint pen.

13 Cut out three daises and press their petals out a little with a modelling tool before attaching them to the initial over the join between the upright and crossbar. Press a small ball of dough into each daisy centre and prick these all over with a cocktail stick (toothpick).

14 Cut out the butterfly, flute its wings and make a body, see page 10. Arrange the butterfly on the initial. Attach one hanging hook in the top and another at the bottom of the initial. Bake at 145°C (290°F/Gas 1½) for about 2½ hours.

Painting and Finishing

● Mix up a little flesh colour and paint the face, arms and legs, see page 24. Redden the knees a little and make the face look more hot and bothered than normal if you like.

When dry, paint the hair, moustache and

eyebrows with a little thin Raw Umber. Paint the eyes with a mixture of Ultramarine and white and the mouth with a wash of Cadmium Red. Take a clean brushful of water and slightly dampen all the items of dress to be painted white, then wash on a thin, but opaque, layer of white. Allow the white to dry before painting the trim on the sweater and socks with one stripe of Olive Green and one of Spectrum Violet. It is easier to keep these lines straight using a rigger brush, see page 26.

Use a mixture of Lemon Yellow and a touch of Olive Green for the tennis balls — do not worry too much if you smudge this colour on the string bag, the Spectrum Violet will easily cover it up. When the balls are quite dry, use a fine brush and paint the string bag carefully with Spectrum Violet.

Paint the daises white and while they are wet smudge a little diluted Cadmium Red mixed with white onto the tips of the petals. Paint the centres of the daises Lemon Yellow, smudged with a touch of diluted Cadmium Red around one side. Mix a small amount of Lemon Yellow into the Olive Green and paint groups of leaves around the daises.

The butterfly is painted with a mixture of Cadmium Red and Cadmium Yellow, with a touch of pure yellow dabbed onto it while it is still wet. Tinge the edge with some pale blue when the first colour is dry and paint the body with Raw Umber, with lines and spots of black and white. Add two white spots, encircled with black on the wings and paint two antennae on the dough just in front of the head.

Paint the tennis racket with Burnt Sienna. Use a mixture of Ultramarine and white to paint the handle and to decorate the racket. The studs around the head of the racket are painted in silver but you could just as easily use white.

· GINGERBREAD ·
MEN AND WOMEN

These rather sophisticated figures are made with biscuit (cookie) cutters; however, with just a few additions, they make quite witty Christmas tree gifts or place-name markers, especially if you can make them look *something* like your guests.

> ½ quantity Basic Dough, see page 6
> gingerbread man and woman cutters
> garlic press
> fine sieve
> cocktail stick (toothpick)
> 4 Hanging Hooks, see page 11

1   Roll out dough to 6mm (¼in) thick and cut out two gingerbread men and two gingerbread women. Lay them on a baking tray, arranging their arms and legs in different positions to give them some individuality and expression.

2   To make hair for the lady in blue, push some dough through a sieve, see page 8, and arrange it on her head in a short style. Make a neat 'bobbed' style for the lady in green, from dough that has been passed through the garlic press; use the same method to make shorter styles for the men.

3   Form two small balls of dough into noses for the ladies and model two small wedges of dough to make slightly more curved or aquiline noses for the men.

4   Give one of the men a droopy moustache and mark a mouth beneath it by making a hole with the cocktail stick (toothpick). Give the other man a fuller mouth by attaching a tiny rope of dough and indenting it along the middle. Give the same man protruding eyes and drooping eyelids, by placing two tiny balls

of dough in the correct positions and indenting them across the middle.

5   Give each of the ladies a bust by placing two small balls of dough side by side on their chests. Place a hanging hook in each head and bake the gingerbread people at 145°C (290°F/Gas 1½) for about 1 hour.

Painting and Finishing

● Add a very small amount of Ultramarine to white to make a very pale blue and then use it to paint two almond shapes to represent the whites of the eyes on each of the ladies. Do the same to the man with the moustache, but make the outside edges of his eyes droop down a little. Paint only the lower half of the bulging eyes on the other man.

Add a little more blue to the mixture and paint blue circles in each of the eyes to represent the irises, then allow this to dry before encircling it with a thin line of black.

Paint a small black dot in the middle of each iris and then draw around the almond shapes on the two ladies in the same colour. Add a few eyelashes to their eyes and paint eyebrows and a beauty spot the same colour.

Paint a far thinner line around the almond shape of the eyes on the man with the moustache and give him some thin, and slightly quizzical, eyebrows. Paint a black line through the indentation across the eyes of the second man to represent eyelashes and give him some slightly raised eyebrows.

Mix up some very watery Cadmium Red and blush some onto the cheeks of all the characters; brush this red across the bridge of the nose on the man with the moustache and on the mouth of the other man. Allow this to dry and then paint the mouths of the ladies with pure Cadmium Red.

To finish painting the lady in green, mix up some very watery black paint and wash this

over her legs. Allow it to dry and then criss-cross her legs with fine black lines to represent fish-net stockings. Paint simple black shoe shapes at the end of her legs. Finally, mix up some pure Viridian and paint a dress with long sleeves and a low, square neck line.

Paint the lady in blue's legs with some very watery Ultramarine. Mix some more Ultramarine and white together to obtain a mid-blue for her off-the-shoulder dress. Add two fine shoulder straps to the dress. When the legs are quite dry paint her shoes in Red Ochre.

Take some pure Red Ochre and paint a long, open, dinner-jacket shape on the man with the moustache. Allow this to dry before painting black lapels, cuffs, pocket flaps and buttonholes. Mix a little white into the black to make grey, and paint the same man's trousers. When these are dry, paint his shoes black and his shirt white.

Paint an Ultramarine, cardigan-shaped jacket on the second man and paint some pure Viridian trousers. When both colours are completely dry, take some more Viridian and some Red Ochre and paint a tartan design on the jacket, see page 28. Mix some black and white to make grey for his shoes and leave it to dry. Paint toe caps and laces on the shoes in a slightly paler grey.

Give all the figures a coat of clear poly-urethane gloss varnish and allow them to dry.

You need such small amounts of trimmings to decorate these little figures that it makes more sense to use whatever you have, rather than buying large quantities of all the items I have used in an effort to make exact copies of these dolls. You will probably find that you already have all sorts of suitable sequins, braids and beads. Nevertheless I include the details of materials below to give you some idea of what you can utilize.

Lady in Green   The frill on her dress and turban are made from very fine Japanese paper serviettes, glued on with P.V.A glue. She has a small piece of Ostrich feather held in place on her hat with a large sequin, and a matching sequin on her dress. A row of very small pearls are attached around her neck.

Lady in Blue   The blue lady also has a frill on her dress made from a Japanese paper serviette, this time it is bound with some gold gift-wrapping ribbon. The same type of ribbon is glued around the top of her dress and she has two gold shell-shaped sequins for earrings.

Man with The Moustache   I have trimmed two small pieces from a paper doily to make the frills for his dress shirt and added three black beads for the buttons. His tie and cummerband are made from fine Japanese paper serviettes and his three coat buttons are black sequins.

Man in The Tartan Jacket   I cut a piece of white floristry ribbon into a triangular shape and folded the top over to make a polo-necked shirt, then glued it on with P.V.A. glue. A small piece of the same ribbon makes his handkerchief, and his buttons are three gold sequins.

FAMILY CELEBRATIONS

As everyone who has ever shopped for the betrothed, a bride or a baby knows, it is almost impossible to find something original. This is when dough modelling can come to the rescue — whether you give it in addition to the main present or on its own, a dough model made especially for the occasion will make your gift truly unique.

· ENGAGEMENT BOWL ·

vegetable oil
ovenproof bowl without lip
1¼ quantities Basic Dough, see page 6
Egg Glaze, see page 7
large heart cutter
about 350 small flat china beads
retracted ballpoint pen
primrose cutter · small heart crimper
medium leaf cutter
2.5cm (1in) round cutter
several stamens

1 Thoroughly oil the outside of the bowl and place it upside down on a baking tray. Take some of the dough and make two thickish ropes long enough to encircle the base of the bowl as it now stands. Make a twist of the two ropes, see page 8, and arrange this around the base. Trim both ends diagonally and join them together neatly with a little water.

2 Roll out half the remaining dough to 6mm (¼in) thick. Cut out sufficient hearts to fit around the bowl on top of the twist. While you still have the hearts loose, dampen the front of them *slightly* with a little egg glaze and press the beads gently into the dough in a heart-shaped design. When you have decorated all the hearts, arrange them around the bowl on top of the twist and with the beads facing inwards. The hearts should be upside down and touching one another. Make sure that you dampen the dough slightly with a little water, where it touches the twist and where the hearts touch each other.

3 Make a finger-thick rope of dough and decorate it with the retracted ballpoint pen before fitting it around the bowl on top of the hearts. Secure it to the points with a little water, decorated side innermost.

4 You should be nearing the top of the bowl by now. Make six balls of dough just big enough to stand a little higher than the bottom of the bowl when they are resting on the rope. Attach these with a little water at equal intervals around the bowl.

5 Cut out six primroses and mark their centres with the retracted ballpoint pen. Arrange them in the gaps between the balls. Make a short pencil-thin rope and attach it around the top of the bowl so that it touches the tops of the balls and the flowers.

6 Cut six thin strips of dough and weave them across the top of the bowl, see page 8, securing their ends to the thin rope with a

Pressing beads into the hearts.

CRAFT TIP

The engagement bowl must only be made over the *outside* of an inverted, ovenproof bowl without a rim. Rimmed bowls have a tendency to trap the dough, making it impossible to remove the cooked bowl without ruining all your work.

Attaching the balls and primroses.

CRAFT TIP

If you wish to use a bowl
with a rim or a lip, you must
use it the right way up and
work *inside* it. This means
that you may also arrange the
border decoration at the
same time, in which case the
bowl will only need to go
into the oven once.

little water. Mark the centre of the outside of
each heart with the heart crimper and make a
design around the larger single rope with the
retracted ballpoint pen. Paint the outside of
the bowl with egg glaze. Bake at 145°C
(290°F/Gas 1½) for 1½ hours.

7 When the bowl comes out of the oven
leave it to cool before removing it from the
mould. Then turn it up the right way and
decorate the top. Make two doves, see page
11, and secure them on one side of the bowl
edge with a little water. Cut out and vein six
leaves, see page 11, and arrange them in pairs
around the edge at equal intervals from the
doves and from each other.

8 Using the 2.5cm (1in) cutter, make three
medium roses and place one in the centre of
each pair of leaves. Fill the spaces between
the roses and doves with flowers made using
the primrose cutter. Place three stamens in
the centre of each flower. Finally, make a very
thin rope and encircle the woven area at the
bottom of the bowl with it.

9 Taking care to avoid any areas which you
intend to paint, give the bowl a coat of egg
glaze and return it to the oven for 1 hour.

Painting and Finishing

● Dampen the leaves with a little clear water.
Omitting the tips, paint the leaves with
thinned Olive Green. Work diluted Rose
Madder into the tips of the leaves so that it
blends into the green, see page 13.

Make up a fairly watery mixture of
Permanent White and paint the doves. Blend
some very thin Ultramarine into their wings
and tails and edge them with a little of the
diluted Rose Madder. Blend a little of the Rose
Madder onto their chests as well and, while
you have it on the brush, use it to give a hint of
colour to the crimped hearts on the outside of
the bowl.

Use the rest of the watery Permanent White
to paint the primrose-shaped flowers and edge
these with a blend of the Rose Madder.

Thicken the Rose Madder mixture with a
little fresh paint and use it to colour the roses,
the circle at the bottom of the bowl and the
doves' beaks. Mark the doves' eyes with some
neat Ultramarine.

As bowls are often used in the kitchen and
may be put down on damp surfaces, it is a good
idea to give them two or three coats of yacht
varnish inside and out.

· BRIDAL COUPLE ·

This is another model where it is tempting to
make the characters look like the real couple.
This need not be too difficult if, for example,
the bridgroom is undeniably short and fat or
unbelievably tall and thin, or if the bride has
masses of curly, red hair and is known to be
lavish with the eye shadow. However, whatever they look like, you can still have fun
by giving your bridal pair imaginative
expressions.

1¼ quantities Basic Dough, see page 6
cocktail stick (toothpick)
2.5cm (1in) and 12mm (½in) round cutters
blossom plunger cutter
garlic press
15cm (6in) saucer
retracted ballpoint pen

1 Take a handful of well-kneaded dough and
make two 11.5cm (4½in) long, finger-thick
ropes for the groom's legs. If you have to
trim the ropes to size, leave one end of each
rounded to form the feet. Set the legs aside.

Engagement Bowl

CRAFT TIP

Even though dough dolls have extremely simple features, it is amazing how much expression you can show by altering their size and position. A baby-faced person, for example, usually has large eyes set far apart with a small nose and mouth quite close to each other. For a more lugubrious expression, you could try making the head more oval, then put the eyes closer together and leave a greater space between the nose and the mouth. Alternatively, you could just model suitable noses when you are making the dolls and paint the rest of the features when they are cooked, see page 12.

Roll out half the remaining dough to 3mm ($\frac{1}{8}$in) thick. Cut out two 9 × 7.5cm (3$\frac{1}{2}$ × 3in) rectangles and wrap them around the legs with the joins at the back and 12mm ($\frac{1}{2}$in) of the rounded end of the leg protruding. Secure the rectangles to the back of the legs with a little water before laying them side by side on a baking tray.

2   Model a suitably sized piece of dough into a ball for the groom's body and attach it to the top of the legs. Cut two triangles with 5cm (2in) sides from the rolled-out dough and slightly round each of the corners with a knife. Arrange these on either side of the groom's body so that they meet in the middle to resemble a V-necked waistcoat and tuck any spare dough around the back of the body. The waistcoat should cover the join between the body and the top of the legs. Place three very small balls of dough along the seam where the triangles meet, to represent buttons.

3   Make a ball for the head and place it on the body, marking the eyes and mouth with a cocktail stick (toothpick). Attach a tiny ball of dough for a nose. Secure two small strips of dough around his neck so that they stand up like a wing collar.

4   Cut a triangle with a 4cm (1$\frac{1}{2}$in) base and 6.5cm (2$\frac{1}{2}$in) sides. Round off the left-hand side of the base before turning the triangle upside down and fitting it over the right-hand shoulder of the model (*his* right-hand shoulder). This piece represents one side of the coat, so pull it back slightly to reveal the waistcoat and tuck any spare dough away behind the body again. Cut a small tapered strip for the lapel and cut a notch in it, then secure it on the front of the coat with a little water. Make the other side of the coat in a similar way, taking care to show sufficient of the waistcoat as this is going to be his *piece de resistance* when painted.

5   Make an arm about 9cm (3$\frac{1}{2}$in) long with a left hand, see page 9. Wrap a 6.5 × 2.5cm (2$\frac{1}{2}$ × 1in) strip around the bottom of the arm for a shirt cuff. Cut a 6cm (2$\frac{1}{2}$in) square for the coat sleeve and fit it around the arm in a similar way to the trouser legs, leaving some of the shirt cuff showing. Trim the top of the arm diagonally and fit it on the left side of the body with a little water.

6   Cut out a 2.5cm (1in) circle for the hat brim. Then model the crown by making a ball and shaping it slightly. Fix the crown onto the brim with a little water, then tuck the hat under his arm so that his hand curves underneath to support it. Make a generous bow tie for the groom, see page 10, and cut out a blossom for his button hole. Finally, give him some garlic-press hair, see page 8, and add a few dough buttons to his coat and sleeve.

7   Knead all the scraps of dough left from the groom into the remains of the original ball. You may have to add a little water, but knead the dough for 2 to 3 minutes until it is pliable and smooth again. Make a pair of far slimmer, 10cm (4in) long legs for the bride. Keep one end of each rounded and trim the other ends diagonally. Place these on a baking tray beside the groom.

8   Make a small oval body about 4.5cm (1$\frac{3}{4}$in) tall for the bride and attach it to the legs so that the diagonals fit around either side at one end. Then give her a little bust by attaching two small balls of dough close together on her chest.

9   Roll out half the remaining dough to 3mm ($\frac{1}{8}$in) thick. Cut out a triangle with a 20cm (8in) base and 15cm (6in) high sides. Carefully cut scallops along the base of the triangle before indenting a pattern around them with the retracted ballpoint pen. Use the blossom plunger cutter to indent a little flower on every scallop. Cut 2.5cm (1in) from the apex of the triangle, then place it just under the bustline. Drape the rest of the dress around the bride, turning the two straight edges under by about 2.5cm (1in) and allowing one side to flow across the groom's trousers.

10 Make two 6.5cm (2½in) long arms with hands, see page 9, and make two cuffs by attaching tiny ropes of dough around each wrist. Attach the arms to the body as for the groom. Take a strip of dough measuring about 7.5 × 4.5cm (3 × 1¾in). Scallop and decorate this strip in the same way as the dress hem, then drape it across the bust and shoulders to form the top of the dress.

11 Make the bride's head as for the groom but do not give her any hair until you have completed the veil. To do this, cut out a circle of dough using the saucer as a template. Cut it in half and decorate the curved edge of one half using the retracted ballpoint pen and the cocktail stick (toothpick). Arrange the decorated half so that one end of the curved side is laying on the bride's head. Drape the rest of the veil so that it flies out behind the bride. Before permanently securing the veil, make some very long hair by pressing dough through the garlic press, see page 8, and tuck the ends of this up under the veil on top of the head. Trail the rest of the hair out across the veil, then secure the head-piece for the veil with a little water. Cut out some small flowers with the blossom plunger cutter and arrange them as a garland around the head-piece of the veil.

12 Use the small round cutter to make about eighteen small rosebuds, see page 11, and arrange them in the form of a bouquet on the front of the dress, placing the bride's hands around them. Add a few tapered strips of dough for leaves and several little balls of dough, pricked in the middle to represent some more tiny flowers. Finally, add two

Bridal Couple

notched streamers of ribbon to the flower bouquet . . . and the couple are ready to be married.

13 Bake at 145°C (290°F/Gas 1½) for about 3 hours.

Painting and Finishing

● Mix up flesh colour and paint the faces and hands, see page 24. Then take some pure Jet Black and paint the groom's coat. Add a little white to make a dark grey for his trousers. Leave to dry before adding black stripes. You will find that the rigger brush will make this

1 quantity Basic Dough, see page 6
7.5cm (3in) round fluted cutter
cocktail stick (toothpick)
5cm (2in) and 2.5cm (1in) round cutters
fine floristry wire
smallest round cutter from carnation set

1 Take a small handful of dough and make two 10cm (4in) long, pencil-thin ropes. Trim one end of each diagonally and make two small cuts in the opposite ends to represent toes.

2 Model a second handful of dough into an oval shape measuring about 5.5×3cm ($2\frac{1}{4} \times 1\frac{1}{4}$in). Lay the oval vertically on a baking tray and secure the mitred ends of the legs to either side at the bottom of it.

3 Roll out half the remaining dough to 3mm ($\frac{1}{8}$in) thick and cut a 20×7.5cm (8×3in) strip. Lay this horizontally on the work surface and trim the bottom edge so that it is very slightly curved. Wet a spot in the middle of the top edge and, lifting the right-hand side of the dough, fold about 5cm (2in) of it onto the damp spot to make a pleat. Do the same with the left-hand side so that you have two pleats facing each other. Dust a little flour along the top edge of the strip to soak up any dampness, then roll the top 2.5cm (1in) of the dough so that the top of the pleats are flattened. Trim off any uneven dough.

4 Drape the strip across the lower half of the rabbit, so that the pleated edge is on her waist. Tuck the sides under and arrange the dough so that the skirt flares at the bottom and fits into her waist at the top.

5 Make two 7.5cm (3in) long ropes for the arms. Cut both ends diagonally as for legs. Fit

---

job far easier. Add white to the dark grey to make the pale colour for the groom's waistcoat and hat. Leave to dry for 1 to 2 minutes before painting the hat band in a slightly darker grey.

Make a large pool of diluted white, and paint the groom's shirt and the bride's veil, legs and dress. Paint the dress last so that it is still damp enough to blend a little pale pink into the scalloped edges. Make pink by adding the merest hint of Alizarin Crimson to the white. Add a tiny bit more Alizarin and paint some of the paler flowers on the groom's waistcoat and his button hole. You could also paint one or two of the roses in the bride's bouquet and some of the flowers in her head-dress.

Take pure Alizarin and paint the groom's socks, bow tie and the remainder of the flowers on his waistcoat. Let the tie dry for 1 to 2 minutes then add some white dots.

When his socks are dry, paint on black shoes with pale grey laces. Then, while you have the grey on the brush, paint the buttons on his shirt front.

Mix a little Lemon Yellow and white to make a very pale yellow for some of the bride's roses and the centre of the groom's button hole. Add small amounts of Cadmium Red to this mixture to make a variety of pinks and oranges for the bride's roses and the flowers in her head-dress.

Take some pure Olive Green and paint the leaves in the bouquet, the buttons on the groom's waistcoat and some little dots in the middles of, and among, the flowers on his waistcoat.

Complete the bride's bouquet by painting the little balls of dough with a very pale green made from Lemon Yellow, white and a touch of Olive Green. Add a little Ultramarine to white to make the pale blue for the ribbons. Then trim her veil and paint her shoes in Gold.

CRAFT TIP

Making a dough model for a new baby can become slightly tricky if the proud mother assumes that you have attempted a true portrait of herself or – worse still – of her pride and joy! One way of avoiding any confusion is to model both the mother and child as animals, but even then, take care that they are of the soft and cuddly kind.

Rabbits, doormice and teddy bears are fine. Cats and even *some* breeds of dog are acceptable, but pigs are definitely taboo!

the diagonal ends to the body and leave the arms out to the side for the time being.

6   To make the bottom of the apron, cut a 5cm (2in) square from the rolled-out dough. Trim two of the corners to make a curved shape at the bottom, then fit the straight edge around her waist. Cut out a circle with the fluted cutter and frill the edges with the cocktail stick (toothpick), see page 10. Use the 5cm (2in) round cutter to cut out the centre of the fluted circle, then use the remaining frill to trim the edges of the apron. Make a few holes around the inner edge of the frill so that you can paint on ribbon later. Finish the apron with a little pocket.

7   Cut a 3cm (1¼in) square of rolled-out dough and attach it to the rabbit's chest to represent the bib of an apron. Make some more frilling and fit a strip along the right-hand side of the bib and over the shoulder. Arrange the left-hand side to match.

8   Cut out a 2.5cm (1in) circle of rolled-out dough and cut it in half. Use these two semi-circles to make a collar for the top of the dress. Model a small piece of dough into an oval shape for the head and place it on top of the collar with the pointed end foremost. Use the cocktail stick (toothpick) to make nostrils.

9   Cut two long leaf shapes of a similar size and model these into ears by curling in the edges a little. Fit the ears on the head. Cut out the lace cap with the small carnation cutter and make several ribbon holes around the edge before securing it on the head between the ears. Cut two long strips with notched ends and fix these under the cap, then between the ears and out to one side of the head.

10   Cut six short lengths of floristry wire and stick three of these into the dough on either side of her nose to represent whiskers. Fix a thin strip of dough around either wrist to represent cuffs. Finish these off by adding a button made from a little ball of dough.

Nanny Rabbit and Baby Rabbit

11 Make a little head for the baby, without whiskers and nostrils, with a little nose instead. Fit the head on a small oval of dough. Cut out a circle of dough with the fluted cutter and wrap it around the baby rabbit to make a shawl. Lay the baby on the rabbit's chest and put her arms around it, securing the paws with a little water.

12 Make ribbon holes around the shawl edge and prick it all over with a cocktail stick. Flatten a little oval ball of dough for the nanny's brooch.

Painting and Finishing

● Mix up quite a strong blue by adding a little white to some Ultramarine. Paint the nanny's dress with this and dry for a few minutes before painting the stripes in a watery white. Keeping the white fairly thin, but opaque, paint the shawl, apron, cuffs, collar and cap. Allow to dry.

Paint the ribbons on the apron and cap, and the buttons on the cuffs in pure Alizarin. Add a little white to the dress colour and paint the ribbon on the shawl. Mix a little Raw Umber and white, and paint the nanny's face and paws. Blend a little watery Alizarin into the tips of her paws, nose, nostrils and ears before the brown is dry. Paint her eyes.

Add a little more white to the brown. Starting close to her nose, paint a wedge shape skirting the upper edges of her eyes and ending at the outer corners of her ears. Use the same brown to paint the baby rabbit, blending a little watery Alizarin inside his ears and on his nose.

Take a very fine brush and black to paint closed eyes on the baby and a heart-shaped nose on the nanny. Paint the nanny's brooch black and her whiskers white.

CRAFT TIP

This model cannot be hung from the highest point, the mother's hat, because that is not in the centre and the model would hang at an angle. Sometimes you can put a second hook in the next highest point and solve the problem by threading hanging ribbon through the two hooks. That would look clumsy here because there is such a large gap between the hat and the hood on the pram. I put one hook in the hat, and a second and third at either end of the grass; so, two extra pins can be used to hold the model straight when hung.

MOTHER AND BABY
· WITH PRAM ·

$\frac{3}{4}$ quantity Basic Dough, see page 6
7.5cm (3in), 4cm (1½in) and 12mm (½in) round cutters
large plastic drinking straw
small piece of kitchen foil
5cm (2in) round fluted cutter
cocktail stick (toothpick)
15cm (6in) saucer
garlic press
small blossom plunger cutter
3 Hanging Hooks, see page 11

1 Take a handful of dough and make a 22.5cm (9in) long, fairly thick rope. Flatten this slightly with your fingers and lay it on a baking tray.

2 Roll out half the remaining dough to 3mm (⅛in) thick and cut out a 7.5cm (3in) circle. Cut this in two so that one portion is a little larger than the other. Put the larger half to one side, with its curved side towards the bottom. Cut the other piece in half. Secure one half on the cut edge of the first piece to look like a pram with a hood.

3 To make the wheel cut out a 4cm (1½in) circle, Then, using the large plastic drinking straw as a cutter, decorate this with eight holes around the edge. Make a small round centre-piece for the wheel with the 12mm (½in) cutter and secure it in place with a little water. Indent the centre slightly with the drinking straw.

4 Secure the wheel to the curved side of the pram, so that half of it overlaps the body of the pram. Then attach the whole pram at one end of the flattened rope. Tuck a small roll of kitchen foil under the unsupported half of the wheel to prevent it sagging. Make a thin

5cm (2in) rope for the pram handle and, curving the top end over slightly, secure this in place at one end of the pram.

5 Using the 5cm (2in) fluted cutter, cut out a circle and frill the edges, see page 10. Use the cocktail stick (toothpick) to prick holes around the edge inside the frill – these will be used as eyelet holes for painted 'ribbon' at a later stage. Carefully fold the frilled circle in half and arrange it on top of the pram as a coverlet.

6 Make a small ball of dough for the baby's head and mark the eyes and mouth with a cocktail stick (toothpick). Make a tiny ball of dough for the nose and arrange a strip of dough and a bow, see page 10, around the head. Secure the head on top of the coverlet and against the hood of the pram.

7 Prepare two 10cm (4in) long pencil-slim legs for the mother and attach a thin rope around each of the ankles to represent the top of her boots. Secure one of her feet to the flattened rope and arrange the other leg so that it looks as though she is walking. Join her legs at the top with a little water. Model an oval body about 4cm (1½in) high and secure it to the top of her legs.

8 Roll out some more dough, if necessary, and cut out a large circle using the saucer as a template. Cut the top 2.5cm (1in) from the circle, then make a mark in the middle of the straight edge. Make two more marks about one third of the way down from the top around either side of the curve. Hold a ruler between the top mark and one mark on the curve and use it as a guide to cut off a section of dough. Do the same between the top mark and the second mark on the curve. Drape this round-bottomed wedge of dough over the body and legs of the mother so that the curved edge is at the bottom. Tuck the dough under on either side and arrange it so that it is

slightly pleated and floating out behind her.

9 Make a 6.5cm (2½in) arm and left hand, see page 9. Wrap a 5cm (2in) square of dough around the arm to form a sleeve. Cut off the top of the arm diagonally and secure it to the body so that the hand reaches the handle of the pram.

10 Cut a little curved strip about 4cm (1½in) long to form the collar and place it around the top of the coat. Make a pocket from a 4cm (1½in) square of dough, with one side slightly curved. Dampen this around the edges and position it on the coat so that it bulges slightly. Then prick around the edges with a cocktail stick (toothpick) to represent stitching.

Mother and Baby with Pram

CRAFT TIP

This model cannot be hung
from the highest point, the
mother's hat, because that is
not in the centre and the
model would hang at an
angle. Sometimes you can put
a second hook in the next
highest point and solve the
problem by threading hanging
ribbon through the two
hooks. That would look
clumsy here because there is
such a large gap between the
hat and the hood on the
pram. I put one hook in the
hat, and a second and third at
either end of the grass; so,
two extra pins can be used
to hold the model straight
when hung.

11 Cut a thin 5cm (2in) long strip of dough for the belt and attach it on the back of the coat so that it folds under the outside edge a little. Make four tiny balls of dough for the buttons and flatten them slightly. Position three of them down the front of the coat and the fourth at one end of the belt. Make two holes in each button with the cocktail stick (toothpick).

12 Roll a ball of dough for the head and mark the eyes and mouth with a cocktail stick (toothpick). Attach a tiny ball of dough for the nose, then secure the head to the body so that it is slightly turned. Make some long hair with the garlic press and arrange this on the head so that, like the coat, it appears to be blowing backwards.

13 Model a small cylinder of dough for the crown of the hat and fix it on top of the mother's head. Cut out a 4cm (1½in) circle of dough and press it out slightly between your fingers and thumbs. Then fold it in half and fit it across the top of the front of the head, against the crown of the hat. Prick around the curved edge with the cocktail stick (toothpick) and decorate the hat with a few flowers made with the blossom cutter.

14 Finally, cover the flattened base rope with grass, made by pressing dough through the garlic press and picking out short lengths of dough. Dot several little flowers made with the blossom cutter among the grass. Put one hook in the mother's hat and one at either end of the base. Bake at 145°C (290°F/Gas 1½) for about 2 hours.

Painting and Finishing

● Mix up some flesh colour and paint both the faces, see page 24. Add Red Ochre to some diluted white to make enough dusky pink to paint the mother's coat. Allow this to dry. Then make up a mixture of Ultramarine and white for the horizontal and vertical, pale blue stripes. If possible, use a rigger brush to do this, see page 26. Allow the blue to dry.

Use a mixture of Lemon Yellow and white to put in the pale yellow checks, painting horizontal and vertical lines in between the blue ones.

Take some slightly diluted Red Ochre to paint the pram and the mother's hat, gloves and boots. Allow these to dry before using some of the pale yellow mixture and a fine brush or rigger to paint the design on the pram and one of the flowers in the mother's hat. Paint the other two flowers with some of the pale blue and pink leftover from the coat.

Use pure Jet Black to paint the spokes and hub of the pram wheel, and the mother's legs. Allow the black to dry. Then trim the wheel with silver, using the same colour for the pram handle and the mother's coat buttons. Paint the centre of the wheel hub with a touch of Red Ochre.

Mix up quite a pool of Lemon Yellow, Olive Green and white to make the colour for the grass and apply it carefully, making sure that you get in all the nooks and crannies. When the grass is completely dry take some diluted white and paint some of the flowers and the coverlet on the pram.

When the coverlet is dry, add a little Cadmium Red to the white and paint the ribbon on the coverlet, the rest of the flowers and the baby's bow. Finish off by putting a little dot of yellow into the centre of each of the flowers.

MOVING OCCASIONS

Dough houses make wonderful house-warming presents, especially if you can actually reproduce the new home.

· HOUSE WITH A · GEORGIAN DOOR

$1\frac{1}{4}$ quantities Basic Dough, see page 6
plastic ruler
2.5cm (1in) square cutter
retracted ballpoint pen
2.5cm (1in) and 12mm ($\frac{1}{2}$in) round cutters
small leaf cutter
small blossom plunger cutter
clay gun
large tulip shaped stamens
cocktail stick (toothpick)
2 Hanging Hooks, see page 11
1 hairpin

1 Roll out half the dough to 6mm ($\frac{1}{4}$in) thick. Using a well-floured plastic ruler and a sharp knife, cut out a 17.5 × 15cm (7 × 6in) rectangle. Lay this horizontally on the work surface, then mark the centre of the top edge and mark both sides, 5cm (2in) from the top. Lay the ruler between the centre mark and one of the side marks, then cut off and discard a triangle of dough. Do the same on the other side to make a rudimentary house shape. Lay this on a baking try.

2 Take a handful of dough and make a 22.5cm (9in) long finger-thick rope. Starting at the point where the roof begins to slope, curve the rope of dough up and down across the width of the house so that it forms the shape of two gables. Decorate the rope with the retracted ballpoint pen.

3 Make a second rope of the same size as the last one and flatten this slightly with your fingertips before laying it on its side and pushing it up against the base of the house. Secure it in position with a little water.

4 To make the steps, prepare three pencil-thick ropes, 6.5cm ($2\frac{1}{2}$in), 5cm (2in) and 4cm ($1\frac{1}{2}$in) in length. Flatten the ropes slightly with your fingers, then arrange the longest rope to form the bottom step, the middle-size rope above it and the shortest one at the top. Place these on the ledge at the base of the house so that the bottom step begins 9cm ($3\frac{1}{2}$in) from the left-hand side.

5 Make a very thin rope measuring about 10cm (4in) long. Loop this in the shape of an arched doorway, starting and finishing on either side of the top step. Use the small leaf cutter to cut out three shapes in the door symmetrically placed in the position of a fan light. Then place another very thin rope across the door just underneath the fan light. Use the back of a knife to indent panels in the lower half of the door and place a small ball of dough in the centre for a handle.

Putting on one of the gables.

CRAFT TIP

I made this house after a trip to Dublin, a city of buildings with blue plaques and the most wonderful Georgian doors. Unfortunately, that idea seems to have got mixed up with a Hansel and Gretel cottage, which I have had my eye on for years. Dough architects are allowed such licence . . . and the woman in the window seems to be quite happy.

Fixing a balustrade.

DOUGH HOUSES

Although making house portraits is not as difficult as it might sound, features like balconies and fire escapes can tax your ingenuity.

The alternative to actually copying a house is to allow your imagination to take over and invent the fantasy home of your dreams. Then you can really let yourself go, giving it every architectual feature you have ever coveted . . . after all it might be as close as you'll ever get to owning an ancestral home!

6 Cut out three sets of double windows with the square cutter: two on either side at the top of the house and one set to the left of the door. Place a single window to the right of the door. Take care when you are arranging the windows, to make them symmetrical and leave enough room on either side of the door for the balustrade. Make thin, flattened ropes of dough for windowsills on all the windows.

7 To make the balustrades, roll out some dough to 6mm ($\frac{1}{4}$in) thick and cut out two 10 × 2.5cm (4 × 1in) oblongs. Arrange these on either side of the steps, securing one end of each on the wall beside the top step and door. Lay the remaining lengths of each oblong along the steps until you get to the last 5cm (2in). Then sweep each one around into coils facing in opposite directions. Secure each coil to the ledge at the base of the house with a little water.

8 Knead any scraps of dough together with a little water and roll out to 3mm ($\frac{1}{8}$in) thick and cut out about fifty 2.5cm (1in) circles. Starting along the gables, arrange these on the roof as tiles. Make a short cylinder of dough for the chimney stack and place it on one side of the roof. Cut out a few smaller tiles using a 12mm ($\frac{1}{2}$in) round cutter and place these around the chimney stack. Make two smaller cylinders for the chimney pots and secure them on top of the stack. Encircle both of these with little balls of dough, pricking each one in the middle with a cocktail stick (toothpick) to make them more ornamental. Then model a little pigeon to sit on the top, see page 11.

9 Make a 12.5cm (5in) long, thick rope of dough for the tree trunk. Split the top 6.5cm (2$\frac{1}{2}$in) in two, then split the two branches in two again to make more branches. Fix the tree in place against the right-hand side of the

house and score the trunk with a knife to make it look more like wood. Cut out about 35 small leaves and arrange these at the top of the tree so that they cover part of the branches and some of the roof.

10 Arrange some clay-gun grass at the bottom of the tree and along the border on the left-hand side of the ledge.

11 To make a flower pot, make a ball of dough, then hollow it out a little with the round end of a modelling tool. Hold the dough on the modelling tool while you run the back of your knife around it, a little way in from the edge, to make a lip. Make two matching pots and fix them onto the coiled parts of the balustrade. Make a smaller one to go in the right-hand single window.

12 Cut out a small leaf and split it lengthways in two to make two leaves for the smaller pot. Secure these in place so that they are leaning over the edge a little, then stick the stem of one of the tulip stamens into the centre of the pot. Cut out about 30 little blossoms and arrange three of these at the top of the stem. Use the others to fill the balustrade pots and to make a little cluster of polyanthus at the base of the left-hand clumps of grass.

13 Cut about ten of the tulip stamens in half and stick them in among the grass on either side of the steps. Model a couple of tiny arms and hands, see page 9, and lay these over the window sill of the left-hand top window. Then make a little head with some clay gun hair and rest it on top of one of the arms. Cut out a 12mm ($\frac{1}{2}$in) circle and place it on the wall in the middle of the house.

14 As the house is heavy, push one hairpin through the top of the roof, just leaving the top from which to hang the plaque and place two hanging hooks under the ledge for fixing

House with a Georgian Door

pins. Bake the house at 145°C (290°F/Gas 1½) for about 2½ hours.

Painting and Finishing

● Mix very watery white and add a touch of Raw Umber to give it a light beige appearance. Paint this on the house walls and balustrades. Add a spot of Jet black and paint the steps and the ledge. Use pure Flame Red to paint the gables, windowsills and door, adding a black knob when dry.

Add a touch of Red Ochre to Burnt Sienna for the tiles and flowerpots, but add quite a lot of water to this when painting tiles.

Paint the grass in pure Olive Green and add varying amounts of yellow and white to paint leaves on the tree. Paint the tree trunk in pure Burnt Sienna. Use pure Magenta for some of the tulips and the polyanthus. Add a little white to this for the flowers in the large pots. Use the colours you used for the tree leaves to paint a few free-hand leaves around the potted flowers. Make some of the tulips pink (white added to Flame Red), then paint the rest pure Cadmium Yellow.

Dull some Flame Red with a little Raw Umber to paint the flowers in the window. Give all the small flowers yellow centres.

Paint the pigeon with the same colour used on the front steps, blending some Magenta into the feathers and even add a little green. While you have diluted Magenta on your brush, paint sleeves on the figure in the window. Mix up flesh colour, see page 24, to paint her face and hands.

Mix some pale blue and paint the plaque. You could paint the owner's name and date of moving on the plaque in white. Remember to paint a white circle around the edge to make it look authentic.

·TOWN HOUSE·

This house is full of my unfulfilled fantasies – I have longed for a house with a green-tiled roof ever since I was a child, and I am still trying to grow a wisteria long enough for it to cascade down the walls of my house. I would also love a balcony; and my Austrian blinds remain stubbornly at the planning stage . . . even the ginger cat is a long-held ambition and although I have got one who visits, he isn't really mine – yet!

¾ quantity Basic Dough, see page 6
plastic ruler
2.5cm (1in) square cutter
2.5cm (1in) and 12mm (½in) round cutters
retracted ballpoint pen
cocktail stick (toothpick)
thin plastic drinking straw
small leaf cutter
small blossom plunger cutter
2 Hanging Hooks, see page 11

1 Take half of the dough and roll it out to 6mm (½in) thick. Using a well-floured ruler and a sharp knife, cut out a 16.5 × 9cm (6½ × 3½in) rectangle of dough. Lay this vertically on a baking tray and use the square cutter to cut out three evenly spaced windows about 2.5cm (1in) from the top.

2 Leaving a space of about 12mm (½in), cut a further two squares below the left-hand windows. Cut one more window in the right-hand corner, 12mm (½in) from the bottom.

3 Take a sharp knife with a good point and use the back of the blade to indent the shape of a front door to the left of the lower window. The door should be 4 × 2cm (1½ × ¾in).

4 Use the same technique to mark a 4 × 2.5cm (1½ × 1in) garage door to the left of the front door. Cut out two small windows in the top of the front door and use the back of the knife to indent panels at the bottom. Mark the garage door in the same way, with panelled double doors each with two windows. Make three small balls of dough for knobs; place one on the front door and two on the garage.

5 Roll a 4cm (1½in) long finger-thick rope of dough and flatten it to make a door step. Secure this in position by the front door. Model two tiny milk bottle shapes to stand on the door step. Cut a thin strip of rolled-out dough about 11.5cm × 6mm (4½ × ¼in) and attach it under the top set of windows.

6 Roll out some dough to 3mm (⅛in) thick and cut out 35, 2.5cm (1in) circles. Fix about ten of these to the top of the house, curving them towards each other sideways so that they do not lie flat. Fix a second, slightly shorter, line of tiles on top of these, allowing the second row to half cover the first. Arrange a third and fourth row in the same way, making each one shorter than the one before. Finish the top of the roof with an ornamental ridge made from a thin rope of dough, about 7.5cm (3in) long. Indent this with the retracted ballpoint pen and decorate the top with a row of little dough balls.

7 Cut out 16, 12mm (½in) circles and make similar roofs for the front door and garage. These should be only two-tiles high and finished with a tiny rope indented with the cocktail stick (toothpick).

8 To make the balcony, roll out some dough to 6mm (¼in) thick and cut out a 12mm × 8cm (½ × 3¼in) rectangle. Attach this, edge on, under the double window. Cut ten, 2.5cm (1in) lengths from the drinking straws and carefully stick these into the rectangle, around the edge, to represent the railings of the balcony. Make a pencil-thin, 12cm (4¾in)

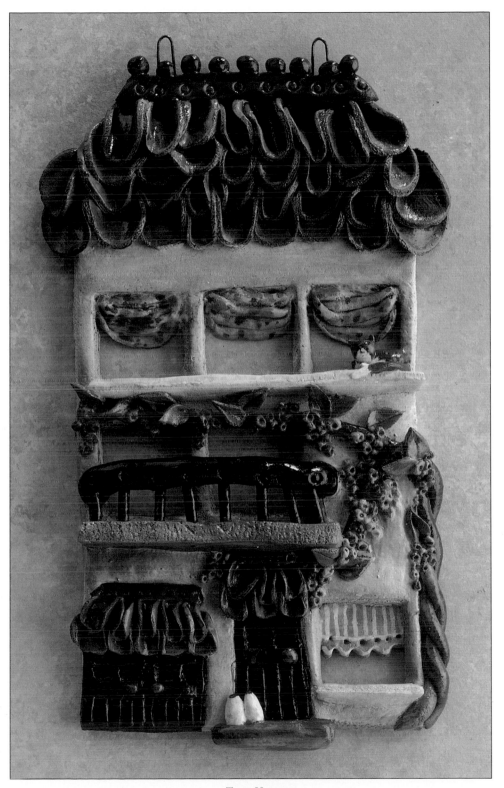

Town House

Fixing on the roof tiles.

long, rope and lay it carefully on the tops of the drinking straws. Attach both ends of this rope to the wall and press down very gently so that the straws become slightly embedded. Decorate it with the retracted ballpoint pen.

9 To make the wisteria tree, prepare two thin, tapering ropes, about 20cm (8in) long. Twist the first 7.5cm (3in) of the fatter ends together. Secure the twisted end of the ropes against the right-hand side of the house with a little water and allow the two tapering ends to drape over and under the balcony.

10 Cut about eighteen small leaves from some thinly rolled dough and indent a vein down the middle of each with the back of a knife. Attach these on the wisteria tree, mainly on the single ropes, at irregular intervals. Make several tiny balls of dough and secure them onto the tree in drooping bunches. Indent the centre of each ball with a cocktail stick (toothpick) to ensure that they do not look like grapes.

11 For the Austrian blinds, cut out three 3cm (1½in) squares of thinly rolled dough. Take one of these and use the cocktail stick (toothpick) like a miniature rolling pin to roll it out a little more. Still using the cocktail stick, push the thinned dough up into folds and catch these together on either side of the square to make an Austrian blind. Do the same with the two other squares. Fit the blinds into the top three windows.

12 To make the blind in the bottom window, cut a 4cm × 12mm (1½ × ½in). Cut a zig-zag border along one of the long edges using the point of a sharp knife. Wet the other edges slightly. With the decorated border downwards, carefully slide this piece of dough under the house and fit it into position behind the window. Make a row of holes just above the edge with the cocktail stick.

13 Make a tiny cat, see page 10, to sit on the windowsill. Put two hanging hooks in either end of the roof and bake the house at 145°C (290°F/gas 1½) for about 1½ hours.

Painting and Finishing

● Add a spot of Ultramarine to some really watery white, and paint the house walls and windowsills with this pale blue mixture. Add a little Jet Black to what is left and wash this over the door step and the balcony floor.

Dilute some Viridian and mix in a touch of Jet Black before painting all the tiles with this colour. Then paint the roof ridges in pure Burnt Sienna and the doors and the balcony in pure Olive Green.

Dilute the remains of the Olive Green and add the smallest touch of Burnt Sienna to get the colour for the wisteria leaves. To get a sort of smudgy, purple-brown for the trunk and branches of the tree, add a touch more brown and a spot of Spectrum Violet to the leaf mixture. Paint this on in a very watery way and allow it to dry before adding the pinks and violets of the flowers.

Make a variety of colours for the flowers by playing with Spectrum Violet, Alizarin Crimson, Permanent White and Ultramarine. When they are dry, give each of the flowers a dab of Cadmium Yellow in the centre.

Mix some Alizarin Crimson and white together to get the colour of the downstairs blind and when this is dry paint white stripes and a border on it.

Mix Cadmium Red and Cadmium Yellow together to make the colour for the cat. Paint some white patches on his face, chest and paws and leave to dry. Then paint his eyes, nose and mouth with black. You will probably find enough bright colours on your palette to smudge onto the Austrian blinds and enough white to paint the milk bottles. Finally, paint the door knobs and the number in gold.

TEMPLATES

Mother's Day Flowers, see page 53

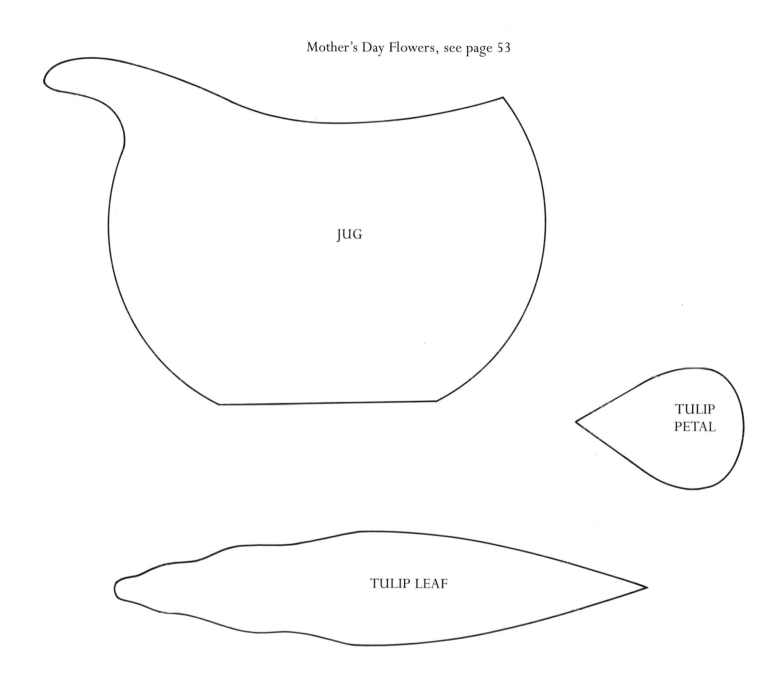

JUG

TULIP
PETAL

TULIP LEAF

TEMPLATES ARE ACTUAL SIZE

INDEX